Nashville
Public Library
Foundation

*This book
donated to the
Nashville Public Library
from the collection of
Dr. Jack M. Batson, Sr.*

Stand and Deliver!

A History of Highway Robbery

David Brandon

SUTTON PUBLISHING

First published in 2001 by
Sutton Publishing Limited · Phoenix Mill
Thrupp · Stroud · Gloucestershire · GL5 2BU

British Library Cataloguing in Publication Data
A catalogue record for this book is available from the British
Library.

ISBN 0-7509-2584-1

To she who must be obeyed

Typeset in 11/14.5pt Sabon.
Typesetting and origination by
Sutton Publishing Limited.
Printed and bound in England by
J.H. Haynes & Co. Ltd, Sparkford.

Contents

List of Plates

Plates 1–6 are between pp. 78 and 79, 7–12 are between pp. 110 and 111, 13–18 are between pp. 142 and 143 and 19–24 are between pp. 174 and 175.

Picture Credits and Acknowledgements

I would like to thank Alan Brooke for his observations, advice and early proof-reading. I am also grateful to my mother for all her encouragement.

I acknowledge the following sources for supplying and granting permission to reproduce images:

Hulton Archive – plates 1, 2, 3, 5, 6, 7, 8, 11, 12, 13, 16, 17, 19, 22
Kobal Collection – plates 23 (United Artists) and 24 (Cannon)
Mary Evans Picture Library – plates 4, 10 and 15
Museum of London – plates 14, 18 and 20
Centre for Oxfordshire Studies – 21.

Introduction

Why is the highwayman perceived as a romantic and glamorous figure? Why have heroes been made out of men who were violent bandits and sometimes murderers and rapists as well? This book attempts to move towards an explanation by examining the activities of some of the best-known highwaymen in England and by trying to describe highway robbery while placing it in its social and economic context. Unlike most other works, it examines highway robbery generally, not just the activities of highwaymen. It covers the period from medieval times to the 1860s, when the citizens of London went in fear of being attacked and robbed by the dreaded garotters.

Mention the word 'highwayman' and everyone has the image of a masked, caped, tricorn-hatted, cavalier-like figure astride a handsome roan, moving out of a wayside thicket, pistols at the ready and uttering the immortal command, 'Stand and Deliver!'. His victims, at least in popular mythology, are well-to-do travellers in their own carriages, on horseback or being conveyed by stage or mail coach. The travellers include a damsel of bewitching beauty who goes into a dramatic, well-timed swoon on catching sight of this menacing yet tantalising robber. The myth continues. The highwayman, because he rides a horse, is likely to be a gentleman by birth. He is gallant and considerate towards his victims, as any gentleman would be. Rumour says that he donates some of the proceeds of his robberies to the district's most needy citizens. Fashionable and wealthy ladies intercede in court on his behalf when he stands trial and visit him in the condemned cell, fulfilling their own fantasies and providing some last-minute succour to the still defiant miscreant about to embark on his awful last journey.

Highwaymen feature in countless folk-tales and ballads, nearly always cast in this kind of romantic light. Novels, plays and films have consistently placed the highwayman in the role of hero, as a dashing gallant or at the very worst, a likeable rogue. Similar adulation is not extended to other highway robbers such as footpads, pickpockets or those now called muggers. How often do we hear of popular songs celebrating the activities of other members of the criminal fraternity such as pimps, embezzlers or burglars? The reality is that many highwaymen were ruthless cut-throats who had no intention of disbursing the proceeds of their robberies to the meek and needy. For such people they had total contempt. They could stay where they always had been, down at the bottom of the social hierarchy. Meanwhile, fortune favoured the bold and so the highwayman grabbed whatever he could and did so totally without scruple or concern for his victims.

The received wisdom that sees crime as antisocial and deviant sheds little useful light on how the common people saw the activities of reprobates like highwaymen. Neither does it illuminate popular perceptions of the nature of criminal activity and of the role of the authorities in attempting to maintain 'their' law and order, 'their' property and privileges while all around them large sections of society went without many of life's necessities. The helpful concepts of 'social crime' and the 'moral economy' were developed by historians such as E.P. Thompson in the 1970s. They denoted the kind of illegal activity that, even if not intentionally, represented a challenge to the status quo and may have enjoyed considerable support from the mass of the population. Most people warm to Robin Hood whenever he gets one over on corrupt and greedy people like the Bishop of Hereford or the Sheriff of Nottingham. Here is the folk-hero, popular because he cocks a snook at those in positions of power and wealth thereby helping to undermine a status quo that the common people know is deeply flawed. Smugglers and poachers are other criminals whose activities have enjoyed widespread popular approval. The 'social crime' concept goes some way towards explaining the selective and irrational nature of popular attitudes towards the different kinds of criminal activity. It is hard to believe, however, that many highwaymen saw themselves as striking a blow against social injustice. The highwayman was there for the money. Many also enjoyed the excitement and the notoriety.

The highwayman may personify some of the aspirations that lie, often well hidden, in most of us. He is a freebooter, a libertarian, a devil-may-care individualist who scorns stifling conventions. Not for him the crushing tedium of a life of diligent but unrewarding toil. His purpose in life was to fill his belly and acquire enough money to enjoy the good life whoring, gambling and drinking with little thought for the morrow, and to do so at the expense of others who may have worked hard for what little they had. In reality the highwayman was a very unlikeable character whose intentions differed little from those of the basest cut-throat or pickpocket also out on the road. For that reason it is hard to grasp why he seems so to have endeared himself to the public.

It undeniably took courage to hold travellers up and highwaymen needed to exude confidence as well as an air of menace and ferocity with which to browbeat their victims. Force of personality could help to avoid the use of physical force. The job required superb horsemanship and stamina because of the need to be out in all weathers and perhaps to ride pell-mell over long distances when being chased. Patience was also needed because the highwayman might wait hours for a suitable opportunity whereupon he would suddenly leap into violent and possibly hazardous action.

Society might have felt some sympathy for the dashing but demobilised cavalry officer after the English Civil War and excused his taking to highway robbery because he had no other useful skill. They did not feel equal compassion and toleration for his subordinate who was a robber on foot, a footpad, a pickpocket or other street nuisance. The highwayman therefore occupies a unique and somewhat contradictory place in that collective consciousness called history.

What kind of society is it that provides the conditions in which highway robbery can thrive? It has flourished in this country at times when the hold of government and of law and order has been tenuous and incomplete. However, society will not have been in a state of complete breakdown, because a prerequisite for the robber was a supply of travellers, preferably affluent, and that required at least some degree of political stability and economic prosperity. Such a situation was to be found in the England of the fourteenth century, frequently wracked by internecine struggles between king and nobility and among the nobles themselves. However, in spite of political and social instability, the country's trade and commerce were growing and there were abundant pickings along the highways for the bold opportunist. Likewise, in the middle of the seventeenth century the Civil War disrupted the tenor of government but continued economic expansion saw traffic on the roads running at unprecedented levels. A factor that partly helps to explain the public perception of the highwayman is that he frequently operated at times when the forces of government were unpopular and enjoyed no real legitimacy. This made it easy to transform a brutal bandit who was handsome, mysterious, rode a fine horse and was outside the law into a popular hero.

The heyday of the highwayman was unquestionably the eighteenth century and Dick Turpin and others of his ilk benefited from the country's burgeoning economic expansion which, however, was well ahead of the corresponding development of its judicial, penal and policing systems. Until the nineteenth century these were appropriate to a largely rural and agricultural society but were proving hopelessly inadequate for a society that was undergoing the traumatic changes associated with large-scale population growth and unplanned industrial and urban development. This was the temporary situation that the highwaymen of legend were able to exploit very effectively until overcome by the economic, social and technological changes that were the product of the Industrial Revolution. By the 1830s the highwayman and his *modus operandi* had become a complete anachronism.

Much that has been written about the highwaymen has been enormously embellished by time and in the telling. The legends that are sometimes the only source of evidence, certainly for the seventeenth century and earlier, provide accounts that are incomplete and with dates and details that often differ. There is no doubt that most if not all of the characters mentioned in the text actually existed and that while there is some basis in fact for the actions with which they are credited, many of the more extravagant details of these adventures can be readily dismissed. They are included for the sake of completeness and because they are frequently entertaining. It should be borne in mind that no official statistics on crime existed in Britain until 1805. A history of highway robbery that dealt only with information that is totally verifiable would be incomplete and probably dull.

Highway robbers were not unique to Britain. The Wild West of the USA has many legendary characters who were bandits or 'road agents' and who held up stage coaches and individual travellers, rustled livestock, robbed banks and even, in a few cases, railway trains. Among the pantheon of such characters are notorious outlaws such as Jesse James, the 'Hole in the Wall Gang', John Wesley Hardin and Butch Cassidy and the Sundance Kid. Australia, too, had its 'Bushrangers', the most notorious of whom were probably the gang led by Ned Kelly. Their activities were similar but they enjoyed the lucrative bonus of sometimes ambushing and capturing large consignments of gold. Europe also had its highway robbers, frequently operating in gangs. In France, Italy and Spain at least they often seem to have combined banditry with rebellion against an oppressive political system or in some cases foreign domination. As nationalists or freedom fighters they may well have used the proceeds of their robberies to finance their guerrilla activities and have enjoyed the support of substantial sections of the population. It is easy to see how they would become invested with the same aura of popularity as folk-heroes, such as that so readily bestowed on Robin Hood.

Few of these robbers, wherever they were, lived long enough to bask in the adoration and respect of their grandchildren. The majority died young and ingloriously at the hand of the executioner, by injuries sustained when their intended victims retaliated or in shoot-outs with the agents of the law. What distinguishes the British mounted highway robber was that he is reputed to have behaved with a gallantry and courtesy towards his victims that is lacking among his equivalents in other countries. He also seems to have gone to his execution displaying a much greater swagger and an open contempt for the authorities, thereby providing a more entertaining piece of theatre. Finally, the British mounted highway robber seems to have been much less likely to kill his victims than his foreign counterparts. While robbery by highwaymen was commonplace enough to be an everyday event, violence and murder perpetrated during its commission were much less frequent than might be expected where the robber's own life was at stake if he was caught.

Much of the material in this book concerns events within the orbit of London and that cannot be avoided given the domination of London during the eighteenth and nineteenth centuries. In 1700 its population was fast approaching half a million, while England's second city by size, Norwich, could boast no more than 20,000 souls. In the period when highwaymen were most active London contained at least one-tenth of England's population and much more than one-tenth of the criminal activity. London society was turbulent and violent with a popular culture based around what would now be regarded as excessive drinking and short-term pleasures of an escapist nature. However, it was not just London's size and wealth that made it the centre of the country's underworld and criminal activity. These provided motives and opportunities for the criminally inclined. Also significant was the cosmopolitan and ever-changing nature of its population, a consequence of which was its lack of 'roots' and of the deference to community, familial and other icons of traditional authority which provided some social cement in the small towns and rural communities of the provinces. London's economy, despite the diversity of its industrial base, was particularly susceptible to economic fluctuations, meaning that much work in the capital was of a casual, uncertain nature, especially among what we would now categorise as the 'unskilled'. London had a large underworld that lived exclusively off the gains of criminal activity but it also contained substantial numbers of people who went to and fro between legal and illegal activity in response to the opportunities available. A substratum of people who obtained their income from criminal activity was, of course, not unique to London but the capital's size and complexity meant that it generally offered richer pickings than anywhere else. For those reasons, robbery around London features largely in these pages.

ONE

The Age of Robin Hood

Some claim for Robin Hood the title of the first English highwayman. As with other English legendary heroes, information about him is dubious and confused and if he existed at all, it was probably in the twelfth or thirteenth centuries. It is possible that his pedigree can be traced back through Philip, Lord of Kyme, to Waltheof, Earl of Northumberland, and Judith, who was a niece of William the Conqueror. Waltheof numbered among his titles that of Earl of Huntingdon, with which Robin is associated. However, some of the ancient ballads refer to Robin as a yeoman and therefore from a humbler estate than the nobility. Here some of the stories surrounding Robin Hood are considered, as are the activities of one or two other highway robbers from the period.

It is asserted that Robin and King John were deadly foes because both were intent on winning the favours of Maid Marian. Her father would have nothing to do with John's avid pursuit of his daughter's favours because the King was a notorious philanderer. Maid Marian is believed to have been the daughter of Robert, Earl Fitzwalter, who is buried at Little Dunmow church in Essex. Legend says that she staunchly maintained her purity until Robin was pardoned so that when he was no longer an outlaw, she could marry him with the full blessing of the Church. The churlish King John, however, is supposed to have been so outraged by the continuing rejection of his lecherous advances that after Robin died he sent her a gift of a poisoned egg, which she unwittingly consumed, promptly collapsing in a terminal swoon. King John has not enjoyed a 'good press' but the story of the poisoned egg sent by a frustrated swain to an unattainable female turns up frequently, and every time with a different sender and with different women recipients. The veracity of these stories may be questioned but the frequency with which Maid Marian appears in ballads suggests that she is useful if only because her presence maintains the romantic interest.

'Robin Hood' or very similar names were by no means uncommon in medieval England. Spice is added to the legends by the idea that he was born into the nobility but was then dispossessed and became the country's most wanted outlaw. These tales go on to say that he was pardoned by the King and had his estates restored. However, such was his love for the greenwood that he turned his back on a life at court and returned to his precious freebooting life. It must be remembered that an outlaw of these times was a pariah, officially repudiated by the law and cast out of the community, being left to fend for himself and to live as a fugitive, dependent on his own skills and a large amount of luck. Intelligent, brave and resourceful Robin may have been, but he was forced to take to the by-ways and forests with little option but to live by illegal hunting and robbery. He appears to have been a natural leader and to have surrounded himself with a band of faithful followers. He also enjoyed the adoration of the ordinary people, who saw him as their champion against the hated and oppressive Forest Laws and all the other injustices and insults that were heaped upon them.

Some scholars believe Robin to be a relic of ancient north European pagan beliefs. A robber with something of the folk-hero about him, and a somewhat similar name, turns up in contemporary France. It has even been suggested by the English anthropologist Margaret Murray[1] that 'Robin Hood' was a generic name for grandmasters of the witch-cult throughout northern Europe and that the name meant 'Robin with a Hood', referring to an important part of the ceremonial attire worn by such figures at the Sabbat. Even if his provenance is accepted as English, then it is puzzling that so many locations appear to commemorate his name. Robin Hood was certainly a peripatetic fellow. His name is obviously synonymous with Sherwood Forest but elsewhere across the United Kingdom are natural features such as hills, bays and tors by which he is commemorated, while innumerable spreading oaks across Britain are also ascribed to him.

Sherwood Forest does seem a particularly appropriate locality for a plucky outlaw who dressed in Lincoln Green and loved nothing better than alfresco banquets of venison, washed down with best English ale. In Sherwood Forest stands the Major Oak, which reputedly was a trysting place for Robin and his Merrie Men. Until a few years ago there was a hollow tree called Robin Hood's Larder where legend says that the outlaws used to hang their venison. The neighbourhood is positively cluttered with Robin Hood associations. Nearby are Fountain Dale, perhaps the home of the saintly looking but roguish Friar Tuck, and Edwinstowe, where Robin and Maid Marian were reputedly married. Close by are Robin Hood's Cave, Robin Hood's Hill, Robin Hood's Meadow and various other places bearing his name.

In the part of the Forest that has now disappeared under suburban Nottingham, Robin is said to have met the King, although we do not know which one, who on this occasion was disguised as a monk. They fought and the King is supposed to have dealt Robin such a blow with a sturdy stave that he knocked him out and carried him off to the court where, rather curiously, Robin was fêted and had his land and titles restored to him. There is no factual evidence to substantiate any of this. However, most kings of the period were obsessed with hunting and it is therefore likely that all of them from Richard I to Edward II would indeed have hunted in Sherwood Forest. The Major Oak and Robin Hood's Larder, however, would not even have been acorns in the thirteenth century.

If Robin existed, did he really spend time plundering the rich and being a general nuisance to the powers-that-be in the Nottingham area? Many early ballads describe him as 'Robin of Barnsdale' and he and his Merrie Men get up to a variety of escapades in this locality, not far from Pontefract in Yorkshire and close to the Great North Road. This would have made it an ideal location for a band of desperadoes who numbered highway robbery among their activities. One ballad mentions how 'Robin of Barnsdale' manages to outwit a sheriff in this area. There is not necessarily a contradiction between Robin being active around Barnsdale and also in the Nottingham area. Sherwood Forest was vast and its northern fringes would only have been about 30 miles south of Barnsdale. We can assume that outlaws would frequently have varied the site of their activities, particularly when there was a hue and cry.

Historians have located a number of men called Robert or Robin Hood or Hod in the twelfth and thirteenth centuries in places as dispersed as Cirencester in Gloucestershire and Wakefield in West Yorkshire. All of them seem to have engaged in activities that were likely to bring them to the attention of the authorities. Perhaps the most likely candidate is a 'Robert Hood', whose name appears in a Pipe Roll. This was an account that had to be rendered by all sheriffs and it included details of tax liabilities in the area over which he had jurisdiction as well as the sheriff's own expenses. The date of this particular document is 1226 and Robert Hood is described as a 'fugitive'. It is not known, of course, whether this is indeed the famed outlaw but it is about the right time and place. The reign of Henry III started in 1216 and lasted for fifty-six years. This monarch successfully used his influence to promote a wide range of progressive economic activities and political institutions, but also presided over an appalling increase in banditry and other social disorders. It may be that in Sherwood Forest or elsewhere a band of outlaws, poachers and highway robbers existed who were well organised and who contained a force of particularly skilled archers who robbed the well-to-do. Perhaps they also acted as defenders of the poor against the more overt depredations of the rapacious barons.

The character of Robin Hood is highlighted in innumerable ballads, some of which possibly date from the period when the outlaw was alive but the majority of which were written in the eighteenth century and later. The ballad was a treasured vehicle for oral history and for entertainment in medieval England. Rather than being sung, it is likely that entertainers recited ballads and it is also probable that the stories grew or altered in the telling. Nobody wanted to hear about a dull, upright fellow with no known vices and so there would have been a natural tendency to embellish the stories in order to make them more interesting and to encourage the audience to want more. Among the Sloane documents in the British Museum there is an anonymous account of Robin's life that states that he was born in about 1160 at a place called Lockesley either in Yorkshire or Nottinghamshire. However, there is no Lockesley in either of those counties and the best we can do is Loxley in Staffordshire, a short distance from Uttoxeter, Loxley in Warwickshire or Loxley in the vicinity of Sheffield, which has various associations with Robin. Another ancient chronicler states that Robin was a Yorkshireman from Wakefield who took part in Thomas of Lancaster's rebellion in 1322. There are many other unsubstantiated assertions about Robin's origins.

It is interesting to note that three separate Scottish chroniclers from the fifteenth century all refer to Robin Hood as if there was not the slightest doubt that they were discussing an actual historical person. Obviously, it is not known what sources of information they drew on but the requirements of modern historiography, which rightly expect historians to provide verifiable supporting evidence for their working hypotheses, did not exist when these chroniclers were active. It is essential to maintain a healthy scepticism about such writings, but this does not mean that they should simply be dismissed. It is interesting to note, however, that there was a popular fifteenth-century proverb, 'Many speak of Robin Hood that never bent his bow'. This could be taken as suggesting that even then there were doubts in the minds of the populace as to whether this folk-hero had ever actually existed.

Perhaps Robin is a combination of bits and pieces, of robbers and rebels who did exist but about whom the stories have changed with the telling. The myth is a very potent one and even without embellishments and exaggerations, it is easy to see how it took root and became part of popular culture. The times in which Robin is supposed to have lived sharply demarcated those with power from the vast majority who had none. The King, the barons and the senior clergy all fought, duped and double-crossed each other in their search for greater power and wealth but were united about the necessity of exploiting the common people and keeping them in their place. As Christina Hole has said, 'Robin Hood was essentially a people's hero.'[2] Perhaps Robin, the man who haunted the thickets, forests and byways of England, accosting affluent travellers and persuading them to lighten their purses, was vicariously the fulfilment of what all the ordinary folk wanted to do – turn the tables on the rich and powerful. Robin outwitted vindictive sheriffs and cunning, greedy, worldly bishops, which was what they would all like to have done. He defied the iniquitous Forest Laws of his day and ate till he was replete with the King's game. He apparently carried out his robberies courteously and happily disbursed the proceeds of his robberies to the poor and needy. That alone would guarantee a place in popular folk-mythology. In addition Robin was healthy and handsome, strong and audacious, a good lover, a man with a mischievous sense of humour, gracious and loyal to his friends. He is a cameo of the person everyone would like to be. He went round righting wrongs, rescuing languishing maidens, hunting in the royal forests, killing and roasting deer for alfresco banquets, all the time cocking a snook at the rich and powerful. It really did not matter that he perhaps never actually existed in this form at all.

Further confusion is caused by the existence of a play and more ballads featuring Robin Hood and various of his associates who often came to be known or at least referred to by the names of the characters they habitually played. So we hear of a Robert Stafford from Sussex whose name appears as 'Friar Tuck' in documents recording the fact that he failed to answer a summons for trespass in the early 1430s. A related difficulty concerns the supposed grave of Little John at Hathersage in Derbyshire. When it was opened it was found to contain bones of the size we might expect of a giant but there is no way to ascertain whether these remains are indeed those of Little John himself. He is supposed to have died peacefully in the neighbourhood although they could perhaps be the remains of an actor of very generous dimensions who played the named role. The Robin Hood plays may have been part of the ancient ceremonies associated with May Day, which leads some scholars to believe that Robin Hood never existed as such but was a surviving relic of ancient pagan practices, a symbolic 'green man'.

There is a strong and persistent tradition that Robin Hood died at Kirklees Priory, not far from Huddersfield in West Yorkshire and was buried in the woods close by. It is said that in his dotage, troubled in mind and body, he repaired to this priory for refuge and treatment. The prioress, despite her conventual vows, was a malicious and perfidious virago working hand-in-glove with Robin's many enemies and, while pretending to nurse him back to health, in fact allowed him, whether by neglect or deliberately, to bleed to death. Robin, realising that he was undone, is then said to have chosen his resting place by shooting two arrows out of the window of his cell and giving instructions that he was to be buried where they fell. One arrow rose high into the air, testimony even at this stage to Robin's skills in archery, but it plummeted straight into the nearby River Calder. The second, however, descended into the park surrounding the priory. The reputed site of his grave is about 500 yards from the farmhouse standing on the site of the priory and containing some remains of its fabric.

It is not difficult to see how the idea of Robin Hood could in time and in different circumstances evolve into a new hero, the highwayman, because the latter had some of the same attributes that made Robin such an engaging if probably illusory figure. The highwayman was to be found on the road, robbing travellers. Especially when they rode in their own carriages, on horseback or aboard a stagecoach, they were likely to be at least moderately well-to-do. Courage and derring-do were needed by the highwayman. Also, because he rode a horse he was probably a gentleman. Was it not part of Robin's attraction that he was supposed to have been a member of the nobility fallen from grace, perhaps the rightful Earl of Huntingdon who went on to turn against the very class that had humiliated and disinherited him? The highwayman too was a 'gentleman of the road' and the fact that he was likely to rob all and sundry and had no intention of distributing his booty among the indigent and deprived people of the area tended to be forgotten.

In considering both Robin and the highwaymen there is the same problem of inadequate and conflicting evidence. Robin's earliest mention in literature seems to be in William Langland's *Piers Plowman*, written between the late 1360s and mid-1380s. In this a drunken priest confesses that he cannot repeat the Lord's Prayer but that he can recite a 'rhyme of Robin Hood'. A more detailed account of his doings appeared from the pen of Wynkyn de Worde in 1495. Those who wrote about Robin, unless they were the querulous Sheriff of Nottingham, outwitted yet again and writing indignantly to Prince John, seem to have done so in a eulogistic style that carried over seamlessly into the general tenor of most writing about highwaymen. This despite the fact that the behaviour of most highwaymen was the opposite of Robin's dashing gallantry.

The ballads certainly portray Robin as a hail-fellow-well-met, a back-slapping sort of a chap, friendly and cheerful to all except hypocritical prelates, shifty, scheming sheriffs with their obsequious underlings, and zealous verderers and forest rangers. Robin was a bandit but the ballads and stories suggest that he loved nothing better than a jape at the expense of such people and took particular delight in duping them with a variety of cunning disguises. He and his men were therefore merry rather than actually mischievous. It is claimed that he never harmed any party that had one or more women in it. It is also said that he was devoted to the cult of the Virgin Mary and made every attempt, in spite of the attendant dangers, to attend Mass. Yet for all this piety, Robin could be ferocious and on one occasion is supposed to have taken part in desperate fighting in the streets of Nottingham during which, with an exhibitionist flourish, he decapitated his arch-enemy, the Sheriff of Nottingham.

One of the legendary highway robbers from before the age of highwaymen is Thomas Dun. It is said that he came from Bedfordshire and lived at about the end of the eleventh century. He seems to have been a gratuitously violent and cruel man who thought that the best way of evading capture was to leave no living witnesses to his robberies. On one occasion, so it is said, he heard that a group of lawyers was to assemble at an inn in Bedford for a social dinner. He arrived at the inn before them and bustled about self-importantly so that the landlord took him for a servant of the lawyers. The lawyers when they got there took him for a servant of the inn. In this dual role he ensured that the meal and the service were of the best. The lawyers were happy to pay for their meals through him and it was only after they had had a long wait for their change that they discovered the deception. Dun had made a thorough job of it and had not only taken the money but their hats and cloaks as well and additionally he had relieved the landlord of some of his best silver. This story turns up in various guises and is simply popular wish fulfilment. Lawyers have never been the most liked of people and ordinary folk would have warmed to the idea of some brave fellow duping them in this way.

There is also a story about Dun and a similarly disliked character, the Sheriff of Bedford. He decided to suppress the band of desperadoes that Dun had surrounded himself with. He sent a large troop of soldiers against Dun's band but they were totally routed. Eleven soldiers were captured and immediately hanged, after having been stripped of their distinctive uniforms. A few days later a group of what appeared to be sheriff's men appeared at the gates of a nearby castle. They said they had reason to believe that the notorious villain Thomas Dun had secreted himself somewhere inside the castle. They easily gained admission, overcame the small garrison and then ransacked the place, removing much valuable booty. A few days later the Sheriff, who had been severely reprimanded for allowing his retainers to commit such an act, hanged one of them who he believed was the ringleader. This precipitated a celebration by Dun's men because it was of course they who had carried out the audacious robbery. This story too seems highly unlikely. Somewhere there is probably a scrap of truth but the rest is embellishment to glorify Dun and belittle the Sheriff and his underlings.

Another hero commemorated in ballads is Gamelyn, who seems to have lived in the middle of the fourteenth century. He was the third son of a man of considerable wealth and was placed under the guardianship of his eldest brother on his father's demise. This brother wilfully misappropriated the estates due to Gamelyn who could do little until he came of age. At the banquet called to celebrate his majority, Gamelyn complained bitterly about his brother's unscrupulousness. In front of the assembled guests, his elder brother mocked him and ordered him to be tied to a post and whipped for his audacity. This seemed to be a signal for all those who had suffered in silence to rise up and give Gamelyn's brother and his understrappers the thrashing of their lives. Led by Gamelyn himself, they did so to such effect that the Sheriff was called in and Gamelyn and his men had to take to the forest as fugitives from the law. They got together with a band of existing outlaws and led by Gamelyn they became highway robbers specialising in holding up rich clerics and thereby assuring themselves of the respect of the oppressed peasantry. Gamelyn heard that his brother was mistreating the vassals on his estates and decided very nobly to take up the case on their behalf at the forthcoming shire court. What he did not know was that his brother had meanwhile been made Sheriff and when Gamelyn presented himself before the court, he was promptly bound in chains as an outlaw. Gamelyn's middle brother Sir Ote turned up unexpectedly and offered his sureties that his younger brother would appear at the next assize. While Gamelyn went back to the forest and resumed his career of highway robbery, his eldest brother set about packing the jury for the forthcoming court case. This blackguard of course handpicked a jury of compliant liars and lickspittles. Gamelyn failed to appear and it looked as if Sir Ote would pay for his gesture of fraternal love by being hanged in his younger brother's place. Just at the right moment Gamelyn and his followers, armed to the teeth, swept into the court and insisted that a new jury be sworn in. They then arraigned the Sheriff, his followers and the displaced jury, condemned them to death for their actions and hanged them. Gamelyn then rode to London to pay homage to the King who responded by making Sir Ote the Sheriff and Gamelyn the Chief Justice of the Forest. Never was there a clearer case of poacher turned gamekeeper.

Both Robin Hood and Gamelyn appear to have come from privileged, landowning backgrounds but not from the ranks of the higher nobility. They are both idealised champions of the oppressed classes and vicariously, on their behalf, frequently outwit venal and corrupt law officers and unsaintly, self-seeking high clergy. One theme these two characters share is respect for the rightful king but hatred of the avaricious barons who have managed to arrogate the right to hunt in the royal forests and exclude from them the poor folk for whom these places often provide desperately needed food. It is in striking a blow for the commonalty that Robin Hood and Gamelyn, to a lesser extent, have been celebrated. No such plaudits were extended to the other gangs of robbers who in medieval times were based in the forests and engaged in rustling, extortion, theft and a range of other activities seen as being purely for their own gain.

Professor Eric Hobsbawm in his acute and innovative monograph on social banditry examines the concept of the 'noble robber', and suggests nine criteria that may be applied when evaluating the lives and activities of those bandits around whom an aura of popular folk-heroism has developed.[3] They are not born to a life of crime but come to it as a result of a miscarriage of justice. They remedy injustices perpetrated on the poor and weak; they take from the rich and give to the poor; they kill only in self-defence or for revenge but never gratuitously. Although outlawed or outcast, they eventually return to an honoured place in the community which, in spirit at least, they never really left. They are admired, assisted and supported by the ordinary people; their death is the result of betrayal; they are loyal to the rightful and just monarch but refuse to accept the authority of petty oppressors. They are also widely considered to have the ability to appear and disappear at will and to be invulnerable.

If Robin Hood existed, he certainly fulfilled most of these criteria but it would be hard to say the same so unequivocally about highwaymen. Some certainly came from wealthy families and suffered the sequestration of their property at the time of the English Civil War but few were philanthropically inclined, many were extremely violent and most died because they were in the wrong place at the wrong time, although some were indeed betrayed. A number of those who operated at about the time of the Civil War were extremely loyal to the Stuart dynasty, the members of which they considered to be the rightful rulers of the country. None of them turned out to be invisible or invulnerable, however, although it did seem impossible at one time to find shackles that Jack Sheppard could not break out of, while Dick Turpin was said to have the uncanny ability to appear simultaneously in two far-distant places. They rarely enjoyed a dotage basking in the admiration of the community, family and friends, although some certainly enjoyed the plaudits of the crowd as they ascended the scaffold.

Popular myths develop a life of their own and as they do reality retreats before rumour. The 'noble robber' idea is highly pervasive and served a need. Robin Hood ballads appeared during the fourteenth century but Robin himself does not become a hero until the sixteenth century. Highwaymen soon found delicious notoriety. By the eighteenth century, women from society's uppermost echelons visited condemned highwaymen in their prison cells and the exploits of highwaymen began to feature in countless folk-tales and ballads. Novels, plays and films continue to appear and usually cast the highwayman in the role of hero, a dashing fellow, a likeable rogue. Rarely are burglars or rapists viewed in a similarly favourable light, yet some highwaymen also indulged in these activities. A particular type of criminal, the highwayman, has been singled out for admiration in this way. Other highway robbers such as footpads and muggers receive no adulatory literature. Even the image of pirates who have sometimes been portrayed as glamorous, swashbuckling characters, is tempered by the widespread feeling that, when all is said and done, they were little more than ruthless cut-throats.

Robin Hood therefore can be said to have his place in a continuum that began in medieval England, developed in Elizabeth I's time, gathered pace in the seventeenth and eighteenth centuries and reached its apogee in the Dick Turpin type of popular hero of nineteenth-century romantic fiction. Vestiges of this process can be descried with the admiration extended in certain circles to the Great Train Robbers and perhaps to a lesser degree to the Kray Brothers.

TWO

Roads in Medieval Times

Robin Hood, according to some accounts, lived in the fourteenth century. It is worth considering both the roads of that period and the travellers who made their way along them. This will help to give some idea of what a highway robber like Robin might have expected to encounter when he and his men went in search of sustenance at the expense of others.

England had a considerable network of roads, many of which dated back to Roman times. The Romans were civil engineers ahead of their time who built an effective system of highways linking places of military and commercial importance. It speaks volumes for them as road builders that many of their works were extant in spite of the neglect to which they had been subjected after the Romans had left. The bridges, however, had mostly collapsed and their successors did not have the technological expertise to repair them effectively. The growing shortage of timber in early medieval England meant that raids were frequently made on Roman roads to extract the stone and take it away for building purposes. That some major trunk roads were maintained in passable condition is strongly suggested by the fact that in 1066 King Harold's forces took only four days to reach London after beating a Norse army at Stamford Bridge near York. They then continued southwards to take on the forces of Duke William of Normandy which had landed near Hastings. However, much of the road system consisted of nothing better than muddy morasses riddled with potholes in the winter and choking dustbowls in periods of hot, dry weather.

When there was a strong monarch on the throne conditions encouraged a slow but perceptible growth in trade and commerce. This brought traffic on to the roads, as did the business of the Church, which was building up its store of worldly wealth. Many priests used the roads to reach scattered cathedral and monastic land-holdings in order to collect rents and other tribute. It was this consideration rather than for charitable or pious reasons that led some monasteries to become involved with road maintenance and bridge-building and upkeep. Useful additional sources of funds were found. Bishops granted indulgences to those who contributed money and labour to road and bridge work, while some toll roads were also established. Additionally, it became a common practice to build chapels on bridges. It was made clear that the Church maintained such bridges and travellers were encouraged to express their gratitude by making a financial offering. Fine examples of these chapels can still be seen at Wakefield and Rotherham in Yorkshire and Bradford-on-Avon in Wiltshire.

Also travelling the road might be richly accoutred and well-guarded caravans containing the King on one of his royal progresses, officials of the Crown such as tax collectors, judges travelling to towns on the assize circuit and sheriffs and their underlings touring the districts over which they had jurisdiction, eminent nobles with their retainers and court messengers. There were also great lumbering wagons and trains of pack animals belonging to merchants and traders, livestock on the move ushered along by harassed drovers, and people, of humble and middling estate, going to and from local markets or travelling to the fairs that were such an important medium for trading at this time. Passenger carriages were few and far between and those who could afford to do so rode on horseback. Other proceeded on foot, slowly and laboriously.

There were other travelling folk for whom the robbers would be on the lookout. Some were virtually highway robbers in their own right.

Prominent among these were the mountebanks and quacks who went around selling what they mendaciously claimed were health-giving, therapeutic and restorative potions, pills and other nostrums.

Other disreputable travellers included the pardoners who could justifiably be described as robbers. The function of the pardoner originated with the Catholic Church's practice of granting indulgences. These were commutations or mitigations of penance for committed sins and had initially involved much hardship. At a later stage offenders were allowed to lessen this hardship by atoning for sin at least partly through the giving of alms and suitable declarations of contrition. In the fourteenth century, the Vatican officially declared that Christ, the Virgin Mary and the Saints provided a repository of goodness and mercy, the benefits of which could be passed on to truly repentant trespassers. This could be done through the good offices of licensed pardoners. In effect these pardoners offered salvation in exchange for cash. It was not long before freelance pardoners appeared on the scene. They were usually equipped with sacred relics and a glib line in sales talk. Chaucer in the *Canterbury Tales* drew an extremely unflattering portrait of one such pardoner whose relic purported to be the sail of St Peter's boat. He clearly regards the pardoner as a confidence trickster infesting the highway and preying on the gullible. Even hardened recidivists made use of the services of pardoners. They continued to practise the worst turpitudes imaginable knowing that they could buy atonement. The trade of the pardoner could be extremely lucrative and it was only in 1562 that they were suppressed.

Away from those roads that were under the control of the ecclesiastical authorities neither the great landlords nor their tenants chose to undertake their theoretical responsibility for maintenance. Sometimes the lord of the manor might fill a few potholes but all too frequently bridges collapsed, trees fell obstructing the way and ruts widened into large, sometimes deep and dangerous pools. Travellers merely picked their way round obstacles and so the route of the trackway tended to become wider and increasingly indistinct.

As well as physical difficulties, there was the constant danger presented by bands of robbers. Although they usually consisted of outlaws, outcasts, ne'er-do-wells and those down on their luck, it was not unknown for the barons, who were really little more than gangsters masquerading behind fancy titles, to organise gangs of highway robbers. Among the most notorious was a band operating around Alton in Hampshire. This gang was eventually rounded up and no fewer than 300 of them were hanged. A gang operating in Lancashire in the late fourteenth century numbered at least 500 men. It was against the threat they posed that the Statute of Winchester was passed in 1285. This required that on highways between market towns, all the hedges, shrubbery and other features that could harbour skulking thieves should be removed to a distance of 200 feet from either side of the track. However, it took more than a statute of this sort to stop determined highway robbers. Most travellers believed there was safety in numbers and whenever possible they travelled in groups. They went in terror of being benighted in the pitch blackness of the countryside, victim to fears of hobgoblins and all manner of frightful fiends as well as marauding robbers and wild beasts. Therefore, they hastened on as dusk approached, listening anxiously for the sound of the curfew bell that announced the imminent closure of the town gates or to catch sight of the cresset lamps that were often placed on one of the town's church towers to provide a guiding light for belated travellers.

The English chronicler Matthew Paris (1200–59) gives one of the best contemporary accounts of medieval highway robbery. The date was 1248 and King Henry III was at Winchester when two merchants from Brabant in the Netherlands appeared in high dudgeon having just been robbed at nearby Alton. They claimed that the robbers were members of Henry's own court and said that they recognised some of them there. Obviously not browbeaten by being in the presence of a crowned head, they proceeded to say that unless they received full and immediate restitution, they would try to ensure that all the English merchants in Brabant would be expropriated. The King was angry and ordered a jury of local people to be assembled and to submit the names of those they knew to be responsible for the theft. This they could not or would not do, and the King, now beside himself with wrath, was with difficulty dissuaded from casting the entire jury into the most stygian dungeon in Winchester Castle. A further twelve jurymen were found and, mindful no doubt of the fate so narrowly avoided by their predecessors, they proceeded to name enough people for an entire robber army, not just a gang. Some escaped into exile, while of those arrested and proven guilty, many were fined but sixty were executed.

Despite these drastic sentences, the forest around Alton continued to be a favourite base for bandits and brigands. In 1260 a gang of robbers had the temerity to attack the King's baggage train and a few years later when Henry III had defeated the rebel Simon de Montfort at Evesham one of his chief supporters, Adam de Gurdun, fled to the area rather than surrender. He used the forest as a base from which to terrorise and plunder the roads and small settlements in Berkshire, Wiltshire and Hampshire. His reign of terror was only terminated by a very strong force of troops under the able leadership of the future Edward I. No popular ballads or folk-tales record the life of Gurdun.

The problems posed by powerful and well-organised bands of robbers became more acute as the fourteenth century progressed. Even monks resorted to highway robbery. In 1317 six monks from Rufford Abbey in Nottinghamshire were charged with having held up and robbed a traveller and demanding a ransom. The matter of highway robbery came before the Commons who stated:

Whereas it is notoriously known throughout all the shires of England that robbers, thieves, and other malefactors on foot and on horseback, go and ride on the highway through all the land in divers places, committing larcenies and robberies; may it please our lord the King to charge the nobility of the land that none such be maintained by them, privately or openly; but that they help to arrest and take such bad ones.[1]

In 1342 merchants at Lichfield in Staffordshire were suffering from the depredations of a local gang of robbers and finding it very difficult to obtain protection. The gang was led by Sir Robert de Rideware and struck such fear into travellers in the area that business at Lichfield Fair was seriously threatened. A posse was eventually organised which caught most of the gang but no effort was made to apprehend Sir Robert himself, a clear case of preferential law for the rich.

The pursuit and apprehension of robbers was made needlessly difficult by the existence of the Right of Sanctuary. Even the perpetrator of the most heinous of crimes could claim sanctuary within the precincts of certain cathedrals, monasteries and churches. Pursuers were prevented from forcibly removing such fugitives on threat of the appalling punishment of excommunication. Within forty days the offender could confess his crime and swear to submit to banishment. He then donned a distinctive white tunic of sackcloth and, carrying a cross, made his way as quickly as possible by a prescribed route to an agreed port where he took the first available ship. There were twenty-two major ecclesiastical establishments that had the right of granting sanctuary for life. This privilege was sometimes abused and the result was that the precincts might become full of idle and shiftless good-for-nothings who expected to be fed and looked after while simultaneously cocking a snook at the authorities. Worse than that, at Westminster Abbey at least, the fugitives used the inviolable precincts of the Abbey as a base for systematic robbery. Just after Henry IV had ascended the throne in 1399 there were indignant complaints that apprentices who had robbed their masters were living in some comfort at St Martin-le-Grand on the proceeds of their crimes. The Right of Sanctuary was progressively reduced through the sixteenth and seventeenth centuries.

Other wayfarers gained their living by their ability to amuse, probably doing more good than the medical men and quacks of their time. They included minstrels, tumblers, buffoons, jugglers and singers. In the almost complete absence of books, minstrels had an important role in transmitting a very loose version of oral history that told especially of the lives of the ancient heroes, the King Arthurs and the Robin Hoods. By the fourteenth century, these legends, enormously embellished, were often recited rather than sung. Minstrels and others played for their dinner and for their ale wherever they could attract a crowd but the rewards were greatest when they obtained admission to the house of a grandee and put on a programme of entertainment.

At the beginning of the fifteenth century the House of Commons specifically denounced minstrels as subversives who cunningly used the medium of entertainment to sow the seeds of rebellion among the common people. Certainly, when they were entertaining their peers minstrels included in their repertoire many satirical songs in which the so-called good and great took an almighty tumble. Tales of Robin Hood would have been in this category. They told how Robin, with insouciant audacity, robbed great lords and hypocritical prelates while showing his practical concern for the poor and weak. From such tiny seeds as these came ideas that were to make a contribution to later radical and democratic movements. While minstrels generally comported themselves with dignity, the same could not be said of buffoons and tumblers. They combined physical clowning and tomfoolery with a ready patter of jokes. These were probably coarse and bawdy and would have made their audiences laugh uproariously. The ability of minstrels and buffoons to entertain and provide some light relief from everyday worries did not concern the highway robbers in the audience. They had a very shrewd idea of how much the takings were and therefore what they could expect when they caught up with the entertainers later on the road.

Others on the highway included messengers carrying correspondence and pronouncements on behalf of the King or other powerful figures. These men who were often liveried moved as swiftly as was possible on horseback, given the condition of the roads and they often took short cuts across the fields. Contrasting in pace with the messengers were the pedlars, chapmen and itinerant hucksters who tended to be merry souls, ever ready to exchange banter and witty repartee with all and sundry while wending their ponderous way, often with heavy loads, up and down the King's highways. Somewhat superior to the humble pedlars were the merchants, perhaps in the wool trade. They mostly rode, although not very quickly, with an accompanying horse often well laden with samples. All were grist to the highway robbers' mill.

The fairs of medieval England were enormously important to the business community and ordinary people, and all sorts of travellers were to be found on the roads making their way to and from these great events. Among the largest were St Giles's Fair at Winchester, Sturbridge Fair at Cambridge, Bartholomew Fair at Smithfield in London and Knott Mill Fair at Manchester. Medieval fairs played a major part in the economic and social life of the nation. They attracted very large numbers and robbers preyed on them on the road and by theft in the densely packed crowds.

In medieval England those travellers who had the means stayed at wayside inns and hostelries, many of which had originally been set up by the Church authorities along the major routes taken by pilgrims. These were not luxurious establishments, even by the standards of the day. Complaints were many concerning the unpleasantness of sharing sleeping quarters with numbers of uncongenial fellow travellers who perhaps snored or coughed all night or were pox-ridden. Another source of acrimony was the cost of the accommodation and food and drink, of gratuities and of the fleas and other loathed parasites that infested these establishments.

The poorest and the very richest of wayfarers sought accommodation at monasteries. These had the charitable duty of catering for travellers and for this reason appealed to the humble. They also appealed to the rich and powerful because, as favoured guests, the facilities and hospitality they enjoyed were greatly superior to what was offered at the inns. Simple rustic alehouses would also be found along the way. These were distinguished by the horizontal poles protruding from their façades usually decorated with some greenery which were the forerunners of today's pub-signs. Brewing was woman's work and the 'alehouse' was usually nothing more than the main room of her simple hovel. It was not the custom to offer sleeping accommodation in such places but a glass of good English ale must have been gratefully received to slake the thirst of a dusty, footsore traveller on a hot, sunny day.

Among the interesting characters to be found by the wayside were hermits. For all those hermits who were genuinely reclusive, living lives of rigorous austerity and piety there seem to have been many others who preferred regular contact with their fellow humans and performed such services for travellers as showing them the way or sometimes providing shelter. Many lived close to bridges and this gave them something of a captive audience, and it must have been a very brazen traveller crossing a bridge who could ignore the supplications of a hermit calling on him for alms. As a result those hermits who had the most prized sites waxed fat and found that they had an ideal existence. No work was required of them while enjoying a steady income and there was plenty of time to swap yarns with passers-by. Not surprisingly false hermits put in an appearance. This development came to the attention of the Church authorities who were forced to issue licences for 'approved hermits' and to categorise all other hermits as impostors and vagabonds. The existence of such unscrupulous pretenders gave hermits a bad name, which was hard on the genuine ones.

It is clear that in medieval times brigands, cut-throats and similarly violent robbers had to compete with other villains who, although employing less violence, found a range of ways of gulling or deceiving wayfarers and depriving them of their possessions. The scene was being set for the emergence of the legendary highwaymen of yore.

THREE

Early Highwaymen

There were highway robbers in plenty who stole from the rich but few with that generosity to the poor that was such an appealing feature of Robin Hood's supposed activities. Instead many robbers had no redeeming features at all and stole from the poor without turning a hair. Many were not only robbers but brutal thugs as well, prepared to assault, rape and murder their victims. In 1333, the vicar of Teigh, a tiny parish in Rutland, abandoned his flock and took up with a gang led by James Coterel. They ranged widely throughout the East Midlands terrifying all and sundry with their gratuitous violence.

Many more examples of anti-social behaviour could be given but those highway robbers who can be justifiably described as 'highwaymen' did not appear until two developments had taken place. These were a steady growth in the amount of traffic moving along the country roads and the appearance of the flintlock pistol. The latter was the latest and considerably the best of a line of evolving firearms with which mounted robbers had equipped themselves. It was both light and reasonably accurate and it added greatly to the menace that was *de rigueur* for the highwayman. It also allowed the robber to brandish his threatening weapon in one hand while easily controlling his horse with the other. By the late eighteenth century the blunderbuss had appeared. This was an ideal weapon for a highwayman. It was a muzzle-loading gun that could fire many balls simultaneously making it particularly dangerous because its inherent inaccuracy was compensated for by its wide and random arc of fire.

While the most common representations of highwaymen show them waylaying a coach full of terrified travellers, by preference it was lone travellers or small groups that were held up. With such victims the highwayman had a much better idea of what resistance could be expected whereas in a coach, especially a closed one, the travellers might be armed and able to give a good account of themselves. A highwayman operating on his own usually approached a coach from the front nearside and kept his distance while trying to ensure that the driver, the guard or both had dropped their weapons. Clearly it was difficult and hazardous for an individual mounted robber to browbeat the occupants of a coach into submission, relieve them of their valuables, keep his horse under control and watch out for other travellers on the road. Sometimes highwaymen shot their victims' horses to prevent pursuit. Kinder ones might merely cut through the girths and bridles of the horses. On occasions highwaymen would tie up their victims to delay pursuit.

The act of committing a hold-up on the highway rendered the offender liable to the death penalty. Since the gravity of the offence was not reduced if carried out with courtesy and decorum, it made sense to act swiftly and brutally and to kill if necessary. By doing so, the highwayman drastically reduced the number of possible witnesses and the likelihood of immediate pursuit. In practice, few mounted highway robbers appear to have killed their victims. Most highwaymen seem to have been anxious to avoid being identified as murderers as well. The possession of a horse gave the highwayman the opportunity to leave the scene of the crime very quickly and he therefore felt less vulnerable than the footpad.

A highwayman was probably more at risk from betrayal by an accomplice or someone after the reward money than from retaliation by one of his victims. Highwaymen therefore needed to be suspicious of all those with whom they had any dealings.

However, some were naturally garrulous and boastful and would treat all and sundry to a drink after a successful outing on the road. As the ale flowed so they might become more and more relaxed or even descend into a drunken stupor. Claude Duval for example, was arrested when in his cups.

Where highway robbers occur in Elizabethan literature the attitude to them is remarkably tolerant. In *Henry IV, Part 1* Shakespeare has Falstaff egging Prince Hal on to undertake a hold-up at Gad's Hill on the Dover Road as if it was a mere jape. Highway robbery also features in *The Two Gentlemen of Verona*, which is set in Italy. Three extremely amiable robbers waylay Valentine, who is wandering along pondering gloomily on the fact that he has just been exiled from Milan. On being ordered to stop and hand over his money and valuables, he breaks into a self-pitying monologue. This so affects the tenderhearted bandits that they forego the pleasure of robbing him and on learning that he is an outlaw and a gentleman, they very sportingly ask him to join their band as its leader.

Little is known about the highway robbers of the period before 1550 but it is certain that they were men of a very different kind from Shakespeare's likeable rascals. Such were Sir Gosselin Denville and his younger brother Robert, who lived in the early part of the fourteenth century. These well-bred ne'er-do-wells had been dispatched to Cambridge to study for holy orders but while they were at the university their father died, leaving them a large sum of money. Eagerly they spent their unexpected windfall on the raffish and seedy delights that Cambridge had to offer at that time. Within three years they were almost broke and only then did they turn their attention to finding a career. Neither of the brothers considered himself suitable for the ministry, nor did working for a living appeal to them. What was more natural than to take to the road?

The Denville brothers joined a gang of desperadoes and launched into a series of robberies during which Gosselin distinguished himself by the sheer brutality of the murders he committed and the malevolent relish he displayed when breaking into convents and ravishing the nuns. The gang grew larger and more audacious and it is said that they even robbed King Edward II on his own highway. Gosselin had a price of 1,000 marks on his head and his younger brother 500 marks. Lesser gang members were priced at 100 marks. The gang members were picked off gradually, informed on by zealous upholders of the law or those who simply wanted the reward money. Eventually, a huge force of Sheriff's men surrounded those that were left and after a pitched battle with numerous fatalities on both sides, over twenty gang members were taken to York and summarily executed.

The Denville brothers were villains of the darkest hue who numbered highway robbery among other dastardly deeds but they are perhaps too early to fit neatly into the category of highwaymen. A later, more plausible pretender to the description 'highwayman' is John Popham who like the earlier Denville brothers, was a 'varsity man. Born in 1531, he read law at Balliol College, Oxford, but found it boring and turned instead to roistering with the university's rakes and scapegraces. Among his occasional diversions was the robbing of travellers on the roads into and out of Oxford. He practised highway robbery very profitably for many years until his wife persuaded him to abandon it and return to his studies. She pointed out very shrewdly that he could make far more money safely robbing people as a lawyer than ever he could out on the road with all its attendant hazards.

As soon as Popham had qualified, his rise was rapid. He entered Parliament, was eventually knighted and moved on to the post of Lord Chief Justice. Phrases such as 'poacher turned gamekeeper' come to mind. To his credit, Popham never made any secret of his past. While serving under King James I (1603–25) it is alleged that a former colleague, another highborn 'gentleman of the road', appeared before him and Popham took the opportunity to chat informally to the man while the jury retired to consider the verdict. The situation was not looking promising for the accused but he must have been a man of some spirit because when Popham asked him what had happened to the old crowd, he replied, in the very public forum of the court, 'All are hanged, my lord, except you and me.'

Another early highwayman was Gamaliel Ratsey born into a well-off family from Market Deeping in south Lincolnshire. He seems to have been an Army officer who, when demobilised in the 1600s, stole £40 from an innkeeper at nearby Spalding, was arrested and, knowing that if found guilty he was likely to be hanged, contrived to escape before the trial, albeit clad only in a shirt. He took up with two well-known villains called Snell and Shorthouse. The trio took to the highway as robbers, noted for their boldness. Ratsey wore a particularly grotesque mask that covered his entire face, terrifying his victims and which was so repulsive that it was even mentioned in Ben Jonson's play *The Alchemist*. Stories grew of how 'Gamaliel Hobgoblin', as he was sometimes known, on encountering a penniless victim on the road would make the quaking man provide impromptu entertainment for him and his friends. One luckless victim, an impoverished actor, was forced to recite a passage from *Hamlet*, while an equally impecunious Cambridge don had to give a learned lesson in the classics to an audience of mocking highwaymen. Ratsey's career ended abruptly when he and his companions were caught and Snell and Shorthouse turned King's Evidence. Ratsey was hanged at Bedford in 1605. It is said that despite his ferocity on occasions he gave some of the proceeds of his robberies to the poor. For highway robbers, speed was essential and the idea that they stood around casually enjoying Shakespearean orations or academic tutorials stretches credulity beyond breaking point. However, a seed was set, the idea of the highway robber with the sense of humour, the man happy to be entertained by his victim while he stole from him.

The Ratseys and Denvilles were ahead of their time. The age of the highwayman proper starts in the seventeenth century. It was in the reign of King Charles I that the so-called 'gentleman of the road', the figure given to us by legend and imaginative literature, really came into his own. This was indeed a cavalier, swashbuckling figure with cocked hat, flowing locks, lace at his collar and cuffs and a black crêpe mask covering his eyes. To be a highwayman he also had to be astride a horse. There were highway and street robbers who plied their trade on foot but they were mere footpads and considered a very low form of criminal life. Some highwaymen did conform to the romanticised stereotype but most were of a much more sinister character and appearance and they turned to highway robbery from a strictly business point of view. Many were inveterate but unsuccessful gamblers who, when faced with unmanageable debts, turned to highway robbery. Some were Army officers especially from the cavalry who upon being demobbed found that the skills they had learned in the Army counted for little in civilian life. Being used to good pay, status and the wining and dining that were an essential part of an officer's life, they found themselves suddenly penniless and without prospects. Desperation might drive them on to the road. In the earlier part of the seventeenth century most of the highwaymen of whom some kind of record has been kept were young men, aged thirty or less. What is surprising is that some of them had plenty of money and, having little need to plunder as they did, presumably relished the excitement.

One such maverick was James Clavel, heir to a substantial estate in Dorset. In 1626 he was arrested as a seasoned highwayman of particular notoriety who had made a speciality of robbing the mail. In his defence, Clavel emphasised that although he certainly had committed a number of robberies, he had never employed violence. He was found guilty and condemned to death but he whiled away his time in jail awaiting the outcome of an appeal by writing poems, including one in which he begged the King for clemency. This was a cringingly obsequious piece of verse but King Charles seems to have been flattered when he found himself being indirectly compared with Jesus of Nazareth. He graciously ordered the death sentence be commuted to imprisonment. Here is a sample of Clavel's verse:

I that have robbed so oft am now bid stand,
Death and the Law assault me, and demand
My life and means. I never used men so,
Yet must I die? And is there no relief?
The King of Kings had mercy on a thief.
So may our gracious King too, if he please,
Without his council, grant me a release.
God is his precedent, and men shall see
His mercy go beyond severity.

Clavel was evidently flushed with the success of his poetic efforts and he proceeded to write his autobiography (he was aged twenty-three at the time) entitled 'Recantation of an Ill-led Life'. As an autobiography this was curious for a number of reasons, not the least of which was the fact that much of it was written in verse and rather poor verse at that. Actually there is very little autobiography in Clavel's 'Recantation' and most of his uninspired doggerel consists of hints to travellers about how best to move around the roads without attracting the attention of highway robbers. Clavel was pardoned, a very rare occurrence. Perhaps he had threatened to write more poetry and the authorities jumped at the opportunity to get rid of him. Alternatively, they may have been grateful for Clavel's revelations about his former colleagues and have taken these into account when considering his fate. We get a fuller idea of the nature of the 'Recantation' from its sub-title: 'A Discovery of the Highway Law, with vehement disuassions to all offenders, as also many cautious admonitions and full instructions how to know, shun and apprehend a thief, most necessary for all honest travellers to peruse, observe, and practice.'

Another young blood, eager to prove himself on the highway, was Isaac Atkinson, again born into a well-heeled family. Even as a youth Isaac enraged his father because of his avid pursuit of female flesh of every description. In this case the sins of the son were visited on the father whose life became extremely tedious because of the procession to his door of fathers all complaining that Atkinson Junior had deflowered their daughters. The monotony of attempting to propitiate them was hardly relieved by rancorous discussions with the many and equally indignant husbands who had been cuckolded by the young man. As the number of Atkinson Senior's unwanted grandchildren rose inexorably and with wearisome regularity, the old man finally decided that enough was enough and he unceremoniously ejected Isaac from the house, disinheriting him on the way out. This proved to be just the break young Isaac had been looking for because he now launched himself into highway robbery with the same energy that he had previously devoted to his pursuit of the opposite sex, although he did not totally abandon his amorous activities.

It is said that the singularly energetic Atkinson held up and robbed no fewer than 160 attorneys in the space of 8 months in the county of Norfolk alone. Questions inevitably come to mind. Why were the roads of Norfolk apparently teeming with attorneys? Did Atkinson rob only attorneys? Was there something about the behaviour or appearance of a travelling attorney that uniquely aroused Atkinson's ire and if so, why? The attorneys provided him with rich pickings because he benefited from these robberies to the tune of £3,000, perhaps as much as £350,000 in today's terms.

Like most highwaymen, Isaac Atkinson's brief career came to an inglorious end. He was apprehended at Turnham Green near London not, as might be expected, lightening the purse of an attorney but stealing a bag of halfpennies from a young and attractive market-woman, albeit believing that it was a bag of gold coins. Eyeing up his victim, Atkinson's carnal instincts, never far below the surface, made him decide to try to seduce her as well. Sensing his intentions, she threw the bag and its clinking contents over a hedge. Atkinson dismounted and went to fetch the bag before giving his full attention to the young woman. Atkinson's stallion seems to have been as libidinous as its master. It took an immediate shine to the girl's small mare which, anxious to safeguard its chastity, turned tail and fled with Atkinson's stallion in hot pursuit. Atkinson was left to rue a bag of halfpennies and a long walk back. The girl, dismounting from her sweat-flecked mare, realised that her riderless equine pursuer signified that the highwayman himself was now stranded on foot. A posse quickly found Atkinson. He gave a good account of himself, shooting four of them until he was overpowered.

At the tender age of twenty-four Atkinson was hanged at Tyburn. He showed little fear and no remorse and merely commented that he had had a short life but a full and merry one. Doubtless innumerable husbands with toothsome wives and the fathers of comely young wenches agreed and breathed a sigh of relief on hearing of Atkinson's premature if predictable end.

Walter Tracey, born in 1596, was the younger son of a prosperous Norfolk landowner. As so often happened, the father wanted his son to enter the Church where his social standing and relative wealth would be assured, but the young man had different ideas. However, he was packed off to Oxford to study theology. At that time there were few places in the country better able to serve the needs of young men eager to sow their wild oats than the venerable university cities of Oxford and Cambridge. Tracey had only been at Oxford for a short time before he fell in with a bad crowd and various misdemeanours led to him being sent down in disgrace. His father threw him out so Tracey found brief employment with a grazier. This was a rather tame occupation for a hot-blooded young rake like Tracey but he enlivened his spare time by seducing the young women of the district. Tracey had charm and good looks and was reckoned to be an accomplished musician and he took full advantage of these gifts in his dealings with the opposite sex. Some accounts of Tracey's life suggest that 'playing on a musical instrument' was a euphemism for sexual activity. Maybe he was a virtuoso.

Tracey eventually married his employer's daughter, having seduced her beforehand, and lined himself up with a handsome dowry and a chance of eventually taking over the family business. Tracey, however, was not prepared to vegetate forever in some rural backwater and he felt the pull of London's bright lights. He persuaded his father-in-law and family to visit London with him but on their way up to the capital he came across some of his erstwhile undergraduate companions. They went off to celebrate this fortuitous reunion with a drinking bout and Walter, admiring the raffish lifestyle of these young men-about-town, determined to embark immediately on a new and more adventurous career. The next morning he stole his father-in-law's wallet and set off for Coventry where he robbed an innkeeper and his wife of 85 guineas. He may have been congratulating himself on his courage and resourcefulness but he had much to learn.

Tracey next met a scholar heading for Oxford whom he pretended to befriend. The man confided that he was carrying £60 with him. Tracey threatened to relieve him of this money but the latter broke down and spun him such a yarn of distress and despair that Tracey gave him £4 of his own money and sent him on his way. Before doing so he had taken the scholar's bag, which he believed contained the £60, and he trotted off well content with the outcome of this encounter. Imagine his chagrin when he discovered that the bag contained nothing more valuable than a collection of verminous and useless old clothes, including a pair of stockings without any feet and a pair of shoes that boasted only one heel between them.

Tracey soon picked up the necessary skills for survival as a highwayman and some years later he is said to have encountered Ben Jonson, the noted playwright, on the road. Jonson's response to being accosted by a sinister figure on horseback pointing a pistol at him was the unexpected one of spontaneously composing and uttering a short verse, casting aspersions on the robber's parentage and predicting his likely destination after death:

> Fly, villain, hence, or by thy coat of steel
> I'll make thy heart my leaden bullet feel,

And send that thricely thievish soul of thine
To Hell, to wean the Devil's valentine!

Far from being put out by this tirade, Tracey rose splendidly to the occasion and proving that he was no mean bard himself, fired back with his own piece of verse twice as long.

Art thou great Ben? Or the revived ghost
Of famous Shakespeare? Or some drunken host
Who, being tipsy with thy muddy beer,
Dost think thy rhymes will daunt my soul with fear?
Nay, know, base slave, that I am one of those
Can take a purse as well in verse, as prose;
And when thou art dead, write this upon thy hearse,
'Here lies a poet who was robbed in verse.'

It is not known how long this exchange of rhyming witticisms and insults lasted, nor whether Tracey succeeded in lightening Jonson's purse. However, it was certainly the start of a bad day for Jonson. A few miles down the road he was attacked by a band of footpads who, like Tracey, showed little respect for his literary achievements and stole his horse after having bound him hand and foot and tied him to a tree with some victims of earlier robberies that day. They were eventually released by some country labourers but not before Jonson heard this immortal exchange between two of his fellow captives, 'Woe unto me, I am undone,' to which his companion promptly retorted, 'Pray, if you are all undone, come and undo me.' Tracey interspersed his activity on the roads with bouts of the amorous activity that seems to have been *de rigueur* for a man in his line of business. Luckier than many, Tracey eventually retired to enjoy his ill-gotten gains. Ironically, his luck ran out when, swindled in some investments, he went on the road once more and made the mistake of holding up the Duke of Buckingham. He was captured, sentenced to death and executed at the age of thirty-eight. His career had lasted longer than that of most highway robbers.

By no means according with the popular image of the highwayman but unquestionably qualifying as highway robbers were Sawney Beane and his family. He was born near Edinburgh in the late sixteenth century and never evinced the slightest interest in pursuing honest toil. Sawney was not only idle but phenomenally repulsive in every way. Fortunately for him, he met a woman just as disgusting as himself. The gruesome duo decided to leave Edinburgh and carve a niche for themselves elsewhere, which is just what they did. They made their headquarters in a complicated system of caves on the Ayrshire coast of west Scotland not far from Ballantrae. They started rustling cattle and then graduated to highway robbery.

Observing the adage that dead men tell no tales and seeking to save on their food bills, the Beanes decided not only to kill the victims of their robberies but to eat them as well. Through a series of incestuous relationships the couple created a family which in due course became a small tribe consisting of eight sons, six daughters, eighteen grandsons and fourteen granddaughters. Rumour was rife and searches were instituted but nobody was able to find the hideaway and the tribe waxed fat on their high-protein diet. Sometimes they had more food than they could eat and they would go to the seaward end of the caves and dispose of a few human remains in the sea. These sometimes became caught in fishermens' nets or were washed up along the coast. The Beane tribe resided in these caves as robbers and cannibals for at least twenty-five years but were eventually caught, hauled off to Edinburgh and summarily executed. They were guilty of three of the most taboo actions known to humanity: incest, murder and cannibalism. Estimates of the number of their murder victims rose to a thousand or more, although it is likely that the final total was considerably smaller than this.

The highway robbers of this period are not generally as well known as many of the later 'gentlemen of the road'. It is likely that the robbery business was somewhat 'hit-and-miss' before economic and commercial growth was reflected in increasing numbers of travellers carrying cash and other items of interest. Sawney Beane of course is not in any way typical but the *modus operandi* of the mounted and armed robber had been established and was to move on into the swashbuckling later seventeenth and eighteenth centuries.

FOUR

Highwaymen and the Civil War

It was to be expected that highwaymen would largely be supporters of the King in the Civil War of the 1640s. Many of them were fast-living freebooters and mavericks who supported the King because he represented the long-established land-owning class from which many of them came. They strongly resented the yeomen farmers, merchants, jobbers, intellectuals and other bourgeois parvenus who seemed intent on destroying a system that had lasted for 500 years or more. The Parliamentary ranks contained many puritanical killjoys who disapproved of the sexual and bibulous pleasures in which many highwaymen and others indulged. They closed down alehouses and attacked many other traditional aspects of popular culture.

There were other highwaymen who had more cynical and materialistic reasons for hoping that the supporters of the King would prevail. Not for them the risks entailed by actually enlisting in the Royalist forces; after all business was business. These gentlemen feared that the dead hand of Puritanism would descend on society as a whole and especially the rich. Those who travelled by coach or carriage were usually well off. To cope with the various discomforts and frequent inconveniences that accompanied road travel in the seventeenth century, many travellers not only imbibed fully at the various halts for refreshment along the way but carried further alcoholic sustenance with them for the between-times. A carriage full of intoxicated travellers was easy game, but

Parliament's forces, strongly influenced by the Puritans, sought to discourage the sale of alcoholic liquors. What better reason could there be for giving moral support to the Royalist forces?

Some of the more idealistic highwaymen did indeed take the King's Shilling. Many paid with their lives, cut down at the battles of Marston Moor, Naseby, Edgehill and the rest. Those who survived and were known Royalist supporters were wanted men, dispossessed and with a price on their heads. Their horses and the military skills they had picked up were often their only stock-in-trade. Where else could they go but on to the highways as robbers? During the Civil War, and even more so during the Commonwealth which followed, the roads became infested with highwaymen and footpads, individually or in gangs. Most were ex-soldiers. They became such a nuisance that large rewards were offered for the apprehension of known highway robbers. This led to many being caught and executed.

Typical of the gentleman highwaymen who paid dearly for their Royalist sympathies was Captain Phillip Stafford who suffered the sequestration of his property by the Parliamentarians and was left penniless. With an understandable sense of grievance he set out to get his own back. He did not discriminate between supporters of either side in the Civil War and held up and plundered all travellers at random, accumulating enough money to retire to the north of England where he eventually became a minister. However, such an existence was too humdrum and he went back on the road, not forgetting to take the church plate with him as he left. He was sentenced to death for robbing a farmer of £33 near Reading. He was something of a trailblazer and popular with the watching crowds because he went to the scaffold with an insouciant hauteur that made him into a role model for successive generations of Cavalier highwaymen. He sported a nosegay and wore a new and expensive outfit bought specially for the occasion. Some of the highwaymen of this period were exuberantly Royalist and Cavalier in loyalty, appearance and in gesture. Captain Reynolds, for example, is supposed to have cried, 'God bless King Charles! *Vive le Roi!*' while he stood on the scaffold awaiting execution.

Captain Zachary Howard was such a zealot for the Royalist cause that on being deprived of his estates and forced to take to the road he robbed only those who were clearly supporters of the Parliamentary side in the war. He was evidently not concerned simply with pecuniary gain because he carried on a personal vendetta against all supporters of the hated new regime. He picked his victims with great care. An early one was the Earl of Essex, a former commander-in-chief of the Parliamentary forces. Despite the fact that the Earl had at least six retainers with him, Howard managed to lighten his purse by no less than £1,200.

As well as steely nerve, Howard must have had an effective intelligence system because he heard that General Fairfax was sending a consignment of silver plate to his wife. He waylaid the courier and made off with the plate and a letter addressed to Lady Fairfax. He stowed the plate away safely and then rode with the letter to the Fairfax family home, purporting to be the courier himself. Asked why he had not brought the plate with him, he explained that the area was notorious for highwaymen and therefore he had left it in the safekeeping of a nearby innkeeper of unimpeachable probity. If Lady Fairfax agreed, he would deliver the plate in a couple of day's time. Lady Fairfax was impressed by the stranger's apparent sincerity and told him that he was welcome to stay the night in the servants' quarters. When all were settled down for the night, Howard tied the servants to their beds and gagged them. He then proceeded into the family quarters where it is alleged he coolly raped Lady Fairfax and her daughter, rifled through their possessions, pocketed the choice items and then let himself out by the front door. General Fairfax was obviously outraged and he offered a reward of £500 for the capture of Howard. This seems a rather miserly sum given the ordeal that Fairfax's womenfolk had undergone. Howard wisely retreated to Ireland until he felt it was safe to return to the mainland.

On Howard's return he really put his head in the lion's mouth. He booked into an inn at Chester where Oliver Cromwell, the Lord Protector, was staying. He insinuated himself into Cromwell's company and got on so well with him that the Lord Protector invited him to his bedroom for prayers. Scarcely able to believe his luck, Howard knelt down devoutly next to the most powerful man in the country. He then whipped out a pistol, gagged and bound Cromwell, seized a few valuables and made good his escape, but not, allegedly, without emptying the contents of a chamber pot over the Protector's head! On another occasion he stopped the Earl of Portsmouth near London when he was accompanied by just one manservant. He relieved the Earl of his valuables but could not resist inflicting further humiliation. He forced him to mount his horse behind his servant but facing backwards and he then tied the two together, back to back. What pleasure he must have derived from seeing the horse trot off with its master's face glowering at him from its unaccustomed and undignified position.

Howard was eventually captured at Blackheath near London after unwisely taking on no fewer than six Parliamentary officers single-handed. After a fierce struggle, he was arrested and incarcerated in Maidstone Gaol. While awaiting execution, Howard was visited by none other than Oliver Cromwell himself. Unfortunately, no record exists of what must have been a priceless conversation. Howard was executed in 1652. He seems to have been motivated by an almost pathological hatred of the Parliamentary leaders. Brutal he may have been yet he was clearly a man of outstanding personal courage. There is no way of establishing how far these tales are actually true. It is unlikely that they are total fabrications but they have certainly been embellished and exaggerated in the retelling. Those who chronicled the exploits of men like Zachary Howard often had an axe to grind. They wanted to write a rattling good story that would sell and put those they disliked, such as the dour, humourless Cromwell, in an unfavourable light.

Another fanatical supporter of the Crown, though of more humble origins, was John Cottington, nicknamed 'Mulled Sack'. Born in about 1612, he was the youngest son of a London haberdasher who drank himself to death and left absolutely nothing for his nineteen children. At the age of eight, Cottington became a chimney sweep's apprentice but he quickly decided that slithering about in sooty flues was not the career for him and he took to the streets as a pickpocket. He proved to be an exceptionally skilled and successful one. Even as a youth he displayed a taste for alcohol, and his favourite drink was mulled sack, hence his nickname.

Cottington decided only to pick the pockets of those associated with the Parliamentary side, and among his victims was the selfsame Lady Fairfax whose virtue had been assailed by Zachary Howard a few years earlier. Split-second planning and timing were needed in order to rob her. Having learnt that Lady Fairfax was due to attend worship at St Martin's in Ludgate, Cottington paraded up and down outside the church dressed in his best. Lady Fairfax's coach drew to a halt and then started to tip over just as she was alighting. A group of gallant gentlemen then rushed forward, Cottington at their head. He rescued her from physical danger and indignity and received in return the sweet thanks and winning smile of the shaken but safe Lady Fairfax. He also acquired a valuable gold watch, which he surreptitiously removed from her watch chain. Ever the gallant, he accompanied her to the church door and bid her adieu with a flourish of his hat. His accomplices of course had tampered with the coach's axle-pin so that it was timed to work itself out and topple the coach just when it arrived at the church.

Cottington next decided to try his hand properly at the highwayman's trade. Hounslow Heath was his favourite stamping ground and he worked the area with a partner called Tom Cheney. One day they spotted a colonel of the New Model Army by the name of Hewson, riding along a few hundred yards ahead of his troops. Without any ado, they called on him to halt and robbed him of his purse. They then turned and galloped away, hotly pursued by

Hewson's men. Cheney gave his adversaries a run for their money but was eventually captured and later executed. Cottington escaped. Even more audacious was his hold-up of an Army payroll wagon on Shotover Hill outside Oxford. Some accounts state that he did this single-handed despite the fact that the wagon had a sizeable armed escort. He seized no less than £4,000 on this occasion and before leaving the scene treated the bemused soldiers to a brief homily on the greed of the Commonwealth government. On another occasion he was arrested and charged with robbery but by this time was rich enough to buy the jury off. Later accounts of Cottington's activities became somewhat confused but he was eventually hanged after being convicted of murdering his lover's husband as well as of highway robbery. The year was 1659. He had enjoyed a long run.

In seventeenth-century criminal cant, a 'prig' was a thief, and James Hind was immortalised even during his lifetime by being made the hero of a play entitled *The Prince of Prigs*, the author of which used the pseudonym 'J.S.'. Hind was the archtype of the highwayman-hero with a reputation for gallantry towards the fair sex and of courtesy towards all those he robbed, irrespective of their sex. Born in 1616 at Chipping Norton in Oxfordshire, the son of the local saddler, he went to work as a trainee butcher. Possessing a mercurial temperament, however, he realised that he was never going to be content selling joints of meat. Disappointing his parents and displaying that blissful certainty and confidence reserved only for youth, he set off to find his fortune in London where he quickly made the acquaintance of various members of the underworld.

Hind became friendly with Thomas Allen who was the leader of a successful gang of highwaymen. Hind wanted to join them but they needed to assure themselves that he had the necessary courage and skill. They told him to go to Shooter's Hill and hold up the first traveller who appeared while they secreted themselves in a nearby thicket to watch how he handled the situation. Hind had no problem relieving a rather docile traveller of the sum of £15 but then to the amazement both of spectators and victim, he gave the traveller a coin back because, he said, the man was destitute. Some of the gang deplored this as cheap gamesmanship and because it might establish an undesirable precedent, but Allen was impressed by Hind's sang-froid and accepted him as a member.

Like many highwaymen, Hind eagerly joined the Royalist side when the Civil War broke out. He enlisted in the ranks but his leadership qualities were recognised and he was commissioned. When his beloved King was executed in 1649, Hind decided to wage his own unofficial war on the regicides. In company with Allen and some of the old gang, he planned one of the boldest exploits in the whole history of highwaymen. They resolved to ambush Cromwell's party just outside Huntingdon but he proved to be better guarded than they had expected and a bloody skirmish took place in which Allen was captured and hanged shortly afterwards. Hind just managed to escape, literally riding his horse to death. Before long he was back and among a new crop of victims was a senior Church of England clergyman who, on being accosted, harangued Hind with dire verbal warnings about what the Almighty would do to those who infringed the Eighth Commandment. This prattling prelate was dumbfounded when Hind rapidly responded with a series of apt biblical quotes about the ungodliness of Mammon and how the virtues of humility and charity expounded by Jesus contrasted with the practices of the hierarchy of the Church. The cleric, in spite of his initial bluster and bombast, was quickly reduced to silence.

Hind continued to specialise in robbing leading Parliamentarians so the authorities viewed him as a major threat, while the public viewed him as their darling. His philosophy was the simple one that you might as well go for the big prizes rather than bother with paltry amounts because the law viewed robbery at either end of the scale in precisely the same light. Hind was even prepared to emulate Robin Hood and he is said to have been generous with poor people who he felt were in real need. His fame grew and his actions were those that help to create legends. On one occasion he found a publican in Warwick being turned out of his alehouse by a bullying moneylender to whom the man owed a large sum. Presumably he knew the publican because Hind paid the money owed and sent the moneylender on his way. A few minutes later, disguised, he took the money back at pistol-point. Whether or not there is any truth in this episode, it has two favoured themes: the highwayman helping someone in need and getting the better of a person loathed by the populace.

On another occasion Hind was seeking regicides to rob but with little success as there were few about. Money was running short and so he stopped the first coach that appeared. To his considerable surprise, the coach turned out to be occupied by a group of well-dressed young ladies. Hind was noted for his courteousness to women. Unashamedly playing to the audience, he spun a long yarn to the effect that he was passionately in love with the world's most wonderful woman but was unable to advance his courtship because of a temporary, embarrassing lack of funds. With Hind holding forth so eloquently his listeners vied with each other to express their deepest sympathy and assure him of their best wishes for a hasty resolution to his financial problems. None of the women could actually spare any cash to help him. The only one who had any money at all was taking her dowry of £3,000 in gold coin to her future husband. Hind silently digested this rather indiscreet revelation. What a shame, agreed the girls, that this money was already earmarked. Hind thought it unfortunate too. A master of melodramatic timing, he now revealed his identity. He had already charmed the women so this declaration was met with a chorus of giggles and knowing nudges.

Hind went on to excel himself. Surely the young lady would not mind lending him £1,000 which would just about see him through this crisis on which the rest of his life's happiness depended? Before long her friends were urging her to hand over the money on the strict agreement of course that it was a loan. How could anyone mistrust the charming and surely misrepresented Capt Hind? Soon, £1,000 richer, Hind trotted off on his horse, offering his felicitations to the young lady for a long and happy marriage and promising to repay the loan fully at the earliest possible opportunity. It was a brazen confidence trick on Hind's part and had a sad outcome, although he neither knew nor cared. The young girl's fiancé was livid about the trick that had been played by Hind and told the girl that unless her father replaced the missing money, the marriage was off. Perhaps she had a lucky escape from marriage to a man of such mercenary priorities but she did not see it that way and, broken-hearted, she remained unmarried for the rest of her life.

In due course, Hind was wanted not only because of his exploits on the highway but also because of his continued support for the Stuart cause even after the execution of Charles I. Nobody could be found to testify against him on charges of highway robbery but early in 1652 they charged him with the manslaughter of a friend he had killed in an argument. He was found guilty and sentenced to death. To the disgust of those who wanted Hind called to account, Cromwell issued an amnesty for virtually every offence except high treason. Those who wanted rid of Hind then arraigned him for treason on account of his blatant support of the deceased King and because he had also rallied to the support of Charles II when he made his abortive attempt to claim the throne of England in 1651. Hind did not conceal his contempt for his tormentors and indeed made it clear that he stood by the support that he had given to the Stuart monarchy. On 24 September 1652, he was hanged, drawn and quartered at Worcester as a traitor to his country. So died one of the most colourful of the early highwaymen. Legend says he was still smiling when his severed head was put up for display on the Severn Bridge.

Hind's life was the very stuff of which legends are made. It contributed to the enduring image of the gentleman highway robber who displayed an impeccable range of the social graces. Once, when times were hard, Hind is said to have stopped a shabby looking countryman driving a cow to market. He admitted having 40s on him and told Hind that it had taken him two years to save the money. Hind relieved him of the money but promised to return to the same spot a week later when he would repay double the sum as long as the man told nobody. Hind was as good as his word.

James Hind may be the role model for the romantic and chivalrous highwayman of legend, but it is certain that for every one of his sort there were far more who were rude, violent and unpredictable. One, a graduate of Cambridge University, is said to have sneered at a female victim who was tearfully appealing to him to be allowed to keep her money: 'You whining bitch, how you throw your snot and snivel about nothing at all!' More serious was the action of Jacob Halsey who, on having deprived one young lady of her jewellery and money, proceeded to rape her. He purportedly uttered these words: 'My pretty lamb, an insurrection of an unruly member obliges me to make use of you on an extraordinary occasion; therefore I must mount thy alluring body, to the end I may come into thee.'

The themes of politeness and gallantry that are ascribed to highwaymen fly in the face of reality. In practice, almost every traveller was potentially dangerous but they were far more likely to surrender their valuables quickly if they met a show of menacing ferocity. Time spent soft-soaping groups of riders or charming a bevy of flustered lady travellers might allow the bolder among them to produce a weapon or slip away in search of help. However, the idea of the courteous villain is deeply embedded in the aura of romance that surrounds highwaymen. In practice, travellers probably extracted little comfort from being robbed by a polite and personable highwayman rather than an ugly, uncouth, evil-smelling and probably trigger-happy brigand on horseback, the end result being the same. It is likely that highwaymen of the violent and charmless sort considerably outnumbered those who were suave, genteel and polite.

The disruptions of the even tenor of life created by the Civil War alongside the continuing growth of trade and commerce meant that these years were fruitful ones for highway robbers. Although some of those mentioned fit the role model for the dashing, gallant gentlemen robber of legend, this should not obscure the fact that many others were uncouth opportunists who made violence and murder part of their stock-in-trade. For every highwayman whose exploits were notable enough to be recorded, there must have been substantial numbers who were captured and ignominiously executed after only one or two forays on to the road. It was not the nature of the highwayman's career for it to end in affluent retirement and in the spinning of yarns and reminiscences for the benefit of adoring grandchildren.

FIVE

Some Ladies of the Road

Highway robbery on horseback required physical strength, courage and aggression, qualities by no means the prerogative of the male sex. Those who argue that anything men can do women can do as well if not better will not be surprised to learn that there were women highway robbers. They tended to dress exactly like their male counterparts, so masks, tricorn hats, capes and riding boots were what the modish lady of the road would sport. They wore these clothes to conceal their sex. How they handled the terse command, 'Stand and Deliver,' we shall never know. They rode astride the horse, giving them a greater degree of control over their mounts. Sitting side-saddle would obviously have given the game away.

Leading light of these women robbers was a most formidable virago, Mary Frith, known far and wide as 'Moll Cutpurse', who was born in about 1584. She was intelligent and resourceful and definitely not the sort to trifle with. Her exact date of birth is not known but she is reputed to have been born with her fists clenched and she quickly learned that with her fists she could command respect. She was adept with the quarterstaff and an excellent wrestler. As a teenager she was described as a 'rumpscuttle', a marvellous word meaning a tomboy or hoyden and now unfortunately obsolete. She grew into a tall woman, commanding in voice and presence and portrayed in some accounts as ugly and in others as comely. Moll was well able to mix with the lads and scorned the company of girls and their domestic and familial activities. As a teenager she was the despair of her parents because of her wilfulness and waywardness. Her father, thinking she would be pleased with an opportunity usually only open to young men, offered to get her an apprenticeship as a saddler but that was too tame for Mary.

Her misdeeds growing greater, Mary's parents in desperation called on her uncle, a minister, to offer his advice. He suggested that she should be sent to America, presumably 'out of sight, out of mind'. They took no chances, accompanying her to the ship and placing her on board. The moment their backs were turned she jumped ship. As they stood on the quay watching the ship drop down below the horizon, massive relief diluted by only the tiniest twinge of remorse, they had no idea that she was only a couple of miles away, marching determinedly towards the blighted rookeries of St Giles in London. She soon proved an adroit pickpocket or cutpurse, hence her nickname, but she was after a larger, more assured income.

Moll Cutpurse set herself up in Fleet Street as a fence or receiver, undercutting her rivals by offering better prices to the pickpockets and other thieves who used her services. She was an astute businesswoman and developed a fast and profitable turnover. What she received from thieves and robbers was quickly on display in her shop and often bought back within the hour by those who had just been robbed. As the fame of Moll's shop grew, those who had had articles valued for sentimental, personal or intrinsic reasons stolen would make their way to her shop.

In a wicked world, Moll gained a reputation for integrity. Those who had been robbed knew that she would not fleece them while robbers knew that they would get a fair price. She was known to be handy with her fists, skilful with pistols or sword and to possess a powerful presence and stentorian voice. Therefore, few people ever gave her trouble and she enjoyed widespread respect. She became an institution, not least because she wore men's clothes, usually sporting an evil-smelling briar pipe, occasionally replacing it with an equally rank cheroot. After hours, she could be found in any of Fleet Street's many taverns, where she was capable of drinking even the most hardened male toper under the table, which she frequently did. The fact that she was androgynous greatly enhanced her sexual attractiveness and she is said to have had innumerable lovers of both sexes. This helps to explain another nickname, and the name of a play, 'The Roaring Girl'. The play in which she was the chief character, was written by Middleton and Dekker and first performed in 1611. Many wished to importune her, but few dared to do so – it was wiser to let her come to you.

Not much is known about Moll's exploits out on the highway but on one occasion she heard that General Fairfax would soon be approaching London across Hounslow Heath. Like many other members of the underworld, Moll found that her income had dropped during the austere days of the Commonwealth and she had no liking for its leaders. In broad daylight she accosted Fairfax who was accompanied by two servants. She relieved him of 250 jacobuses, a gold coin worth between 20 and 25s, but in order to effect a getaway she had to shoot General Fairfax in the arm and the horses from under the servants. Riding pell-mell back towards London, her horse collapsed at Turnham Green and she was quickly captured. Money talked and she was able to obtain her freedom at a cost of at least £2,000. By that time Moll was well-off and could afford it. She died in 1659 of dropsy and in her will left £20 to her drinking associates to spend on celebrating the restoration of the monarchy, something she obviously felt was bound to happen sooner or later. It is likely that for £20 they would have been able to enjoy a carousal that lived on in the memory for a very long time.

Moll may have been eye-catching rather than pleasing to the eye but the word alluring definitely fits Joan Philips, better known as Joan Bracey. She was born in 1656 into comfortable yeoman stock in Northamptonshire, but on starting an affair with a well-known highwayman was ejected peremptorily from the family home. She became his common-law wife and adopted his surname of Bracey.

The couple ran an inn in the West Country where Joan's beauty was an asset because the bar was always full of men eager to eye up, woo and hopefully seduce the exceptionally winsome landlady. Joan's fidelity, however, seemed absolutely unassailable. This naturally only succeeded in making her even more captivating to the lecherous swains who daily jostled each other while leering over the bar of the Braceys' hostelry.

On one occasion one of Joan's suitors proved more persistent than most. Dacey was known to be extremely rich and he thought that perhaps it was his wealth that made her seem to waver from her previous unstinting fidelity. Indeed it certainly was his wealth that caused the apparent change in Joan's response but not for the reason he thought. It was money she was after, not his body. The artless victim could scarcely believe his luck when Joan intimated that he should return to the inn at a time when her husband would be many miles away.

It was a dark night after closing time when Dacey, dressed in his best finery and smelling strongly of scented water, knocked, almost beside himself with anticipation, at the inn door. He was greeted by a maid who took his hand and led him upstairs. Her mistress was waiting eagerly for him in her bedroom, the maid said, but wanted her paramour to undress in a room close by, just in case her husband should return unexpectedly. Dacey thought this seemed sensible but was surprised when the maid herself began avidly taking his clothes off in the dark. He was down to nothing else but a shirt when she whispered that she would take his clothes into another room and then return for him. This she quickly did and, grasping his hand because it was pitch black in the inn, she led him to her mistress's chamber, or at least so he thought. A door opened and he was on his own and surprised to hear the key turn in the lock. He groped around in the darkness trying to locate the bed and calling out his beloved's name. A frisson of expectation scintillated through his body as Joan's disembodied voice told him to locate the door in the other wall. He did so, opened the door and went through it. He then heard the door close and lock while Joan's voice, more muffled this time, told him to continue along the passage and through the door and out into the yard. When he protested that he was undressed, Joan told him that he had his shirt and if he wanted to wait around, her husband would be back in an hour or two. He could then explain to him why he was hanging around outside the inn in the middle of the night clad only in a shirt. Dacey, crestfallen, slunk away, robbed of his pride, his expected prize of the night, his gold watch and chain and other valuables. The inn lost a regular customer that night but the Braceys were laughing.

Sometimes the Braceys worked the roads together but on at least one occasion Joan went out on her own. She held up a coach near Nottingham and had just called on its occupant to deliver when the latter unexpectedly leapt out and knocked her off her horse. She was easily caught and handed over to the authorities who were amazed when the secret of her sex was revealed. She was hanged in 1685 at Nottingham aged just twenty-nine.

Another apparent female robber was Mary Blacket, who could match neither of the other heroines for ugliness or beauty. She was arrested in 1726 for highway robbery and sentenced to be hanged at Tyburn, but what made the case interesting was that she claimed mistaken identity. That was a frequent occurrence but less common was the vehement way in which the normally very placid Mary continued arguing her innocence even when all possibility of a reprieve had been exhausted. She won widespread admiration for the way in which she met her end with consummate dignity. Not showing a hint of fear, she used the scaffold once more to assert her innocence and to declare that she forgave all those who had mistakenly brought her to her death. It seems likely that Mary Blacket was hanged for the crimes of some other, unknown miscreant.

An interesting example of female criminality was Ann Meders, who included fraud and bigamy in her portfolio alongside highway robbery. She seems to have been born in 1643 and grew into a pretty woman obsessed with the idea of achieving high social and financial status. This in itself was not particularly unusual but what marked her out were the methods she employed in pursuit of these aims. Marriage to a wealthy man was one option but she seems to have married three in quick succession without concerning herself overmuch about dissolving the marriages once it became clear that they were not going to provide the instant riches that she craved. This activity attracted the attention of the authorities and Ann withdrew to the continent for a while. Both there and on her return to England she worked her way through large numbers of lovers, many of whom showered her with gifts and money in exchange for sharing her bed. This was exhausting work, physically and emotionally. She was harried by lovelorn or indignant ex-lovers for whom she no longer had any use, pestered by her current tranche of ardent paramours and constantly looking out for fresh admirers prepared to lavish their largesse on her.

Ann's problem was that it did not really seem to matter how much money she received, she was always broke, given the ostentatious lifestyle on which she insisted. One night an old but affluent lover unwisely revealed that he had £200 hidden in his coach. When he left her, she took her own coachman into her confidence and together they sped after him, holding him up at pistol-point. They extorted the money easily, assisted by the threat that if he told the authorities she would personally and immediately tell his wife about the affair and would provide her with the fullest and most scurrilous details of his sexual preferences.

Ann proceeded to carry out many other robberies within the built up area of London but she was eventually arrested for stealing a fine silver plate. Her debut at the Old Bailey was something of a sensation because of the low-cut dress she chose to wear for the occasion. Ann revealed much of her capacious bosom and it probably attracted more attention than the presentation of evidence and other humdrum proceedings of the court. Despite her natural advantages, however, the situation looked bad for Ann so she then used another tactic frequently employed by women who found themselves in the dock – she claimed she was pregnant. A new jury of women was sworn in but with a marked lack of sympathy, they quickly decided that her claim was false. Ann was hanged at Tyburn in January 1673, aged thirty.

In 1662 another female highway robber was born in Ipswich, Suffolk – Nan Hereford. She went into service in London at the age of seventeen and, like many before her, got into bad company in the capital and became involved with a gang of street thieves. She operated as a shoplifter and pickpocket before graduating to working with a male partner named Kirkham. They held up rich and severely inebriated gentlemen staggering back home from their clubs. The attraction of this palled and they decided to try their hand at the highwayman's trade. Kirkham's career as a highwayman was short-lived. He was caught carrying out his very first robbery and was hanged at Tyburn. Nan, however, decided to go it alone and her career in the saddle lasted for about six years.

There are cases of highway robbers inadvertently accosting travellers on the road only to find that the timid horseman turns out to be one of their own kind. This coincidence happened to Margaret Matthews, born in Suffolk in about 1660, and she chose as her 'victim' probably one of the most feared highwayman in East Anglia at the time. He was Thomas Rumbold and he did not take kindly to what appeared to be a slim and callow youth working his patch. Margaret and Rumbold exchanged fire but only managed to hit each other's horses. These collapsed and their riders both fell to the ground. They then continued their argument with swords and eventually Rumbold overcame his adversary and bound his arms and legs. He proceeded to give his vanquished opponent a thorough search to ascertain what valuables he had about his person. He was amazed while rummaging conscientiously through his antagonist's clothing to discover that his captive was female. Such a tantalising discovery would have caused many men to renew their investigations with even greater thoroughness but Rumbold refused to take advantage of the situation and treated Margaret with great consideration, given the circumstances.

Not much is known of the life and activities of Margaret Matthews but she should be credited with the unique achievement of robbing her own husband out on the highway. He had systematically beaten her up and this was one reason why she turned to robbery because she hoped to gain her financial independence. Disguised, she waylaid him in a remote spot knowing that he was carrying a large sum of money. His pitiable fear when faced with what he believed was a highwayman convinced her that, although within the home he was quick with his fists, like so many of his kind he was actually a weak coward.

One female robber who became very famous was Lady Catherine Ferrers, born in 1662. She was the daughter of a well-to-do Hertfordshire landowner who wanted to add social status to his wealth by marrying his daughter to Sir Ralph Ferrers of nearby Markyate Cell. At the age of sixteen, Catherine reluctantly obeyed her father's wishes and married Sir Ralph who was much older and and who proved to be something of a disappointment. In spite of Catherine's strikingly attractive appearance, he seemed more concerned with the stewardship of his estates. Life was too dull for a spirited young woman like Catherine and so, casting around for some spice in her life, she resolved to try her hand at highway robbery. She made use of a secret passage from her bedroom in order to leave home unnoticed. Necessarily she took great pains with her disguise and found, to her delight, that her first victim was none other than her sister-in-law, a bitter shrew of a woman whom she absolutely loathed. Robbery and revenge made a sweet combination.

Catherine Ferrers's first experience gave her the taste for more. She enjoyed the sense of power she obtained from seeing men lose their bluster when facing the business end of a pistol. She extended her range of operations to the busy and potentially lucrative Watling Street that ran close by her home. Her career on the road could have come to an early end when she held up a solitary rider and found herself gazing at a pistol instead. She had accosted a celebrated highwayman by the name of Jerry Jackson. Fortunately, he either saw the funny side of the situation or was perhaps so taken by Catherine's looks when he discovered her sex that he happily put his pistol away. Soon she and Jackson became lovers and partners-in-crime. They worked together for a while, during which time Catherine added murder to her portfolio of misdemeanours. Her partner was eventually captured and hanged at Tyburn. How Catherine ended her career is uncertain but she died in 1684, perhaps from wounds sustained during a robbery or on the gallows. Whatever her fate, the image of such a swashbuckling and nubile highwaywoman was very attractive to filmmakers. The adventures of Catherine Ferrers, or at least a version of them based very loosely on her real life, have been the subject of two films, both of which were entitled *The Wicked Lady*.

The records confirm that most of the women highway robbers mentioned here were hanged but there is a record of one, Mary Pile, who sailed with the first fleet of transported convicts to Botany Bay in 1785. As with their male counterparts, the ladies of the road mostly had short careers which ended predictably in a brief and one-sided meeting with the hangman.

SIX

The Highways of England Before the Industrial Revolution

Contemporary accounts from the medieval period to the eighteenth century provide vivid descriptions of the hazards of road travel in England. Many of these concern the state of the roads themselves. In 1555 the first Highway Act was passed. This made each parish responsible for the upkeep of the roads within its own boundaries. Little improvement took place because many parishes resented spending money to better roads that were used almost exclusively by travellers passing through the district and doing little or nothing for the local economy. Also a system was brought in whereby local labourers were required to spend six days each year repairing the local roads. This enforced work, known as statute labour, was unpaid and performed, if at all, grudgingly and carelessly. In 1654 Parliament allowed parishes to levy rates to employ surveyors to supervise the work. This resulted in some small improvements in road surfaces but these were increasingly negated by the growing number of vehicles with narrow wheels that seriously damaged the road surface, especially in areas of clay soil and in periods of wet weather. Parliament then turned its attention to measures intended to cut down on the use of such vehicles and to encourage those with considerably wider wheels which it was hoped would help to roll and flatten the road surfaces.

The poor condition of the roads during this period proved an advantage to the highwaymen because it reduced coaches and carriages to speeds of 4 or 5 miles per hour, which made their interception comparatively easy. Road travellers of the time constantly bemoaned both the conditions of the roads and the prevalence of highway robbery. The frequency of complaints raises the question of what the authorities were doing about it. The answer is very little. Although the country's highways were theoretically under the suzerainty of the Crown, the citizens of each hundred (the sub-division of a county) could be called to account for all offences committed during daylight hours on the roads in their area. The sum involved in such a robbery had to be a considerable one and the claim for compensation needed to be lodged before sunset on the day of the crime. The authorities had to produce the body of the offender, alive or dead, within forty days of a robbery, and if unable to do so they were collectively fined to make up the cost of what was stolen, which was then given to the victim. In the middle of the sixteenth century this collective indemnity was reduced to 50 per cent of the traveller's loss, clearly indicating that the system was not working effectively. In the same century the Sunday Trading Act removed the liability incurred for hundreds of offences that took place on Sundays, probably because Sunday travelling was seen as something unnecessary and even as morally reprehensible.

The Statute of Winchester in 1285 had been aimed at curbing the activities of highway robbers, mostly footpads, but was largely ineffective against them. Although the nuisance created by footpads should not be underestimated, the emergence of the highwayman was clearly seen as an altogether more serious issue. More and more travellers were using the roads, reflecting the country's industrial and commercial development. The total value of what was being stolen increased steadily and the hundreds were unable to pay up in full, so those who were robbed faced fewer and fewer chances of getting adequate compensation. Incidentally, the law clearly distinguished between robbery during daylight hours and robbery at night. The hundreds had no obligation whatever to recompense travellers who were foolish enough to find themselves robbed during the hours of darkness.

A host of contemporary writers found road travel and its attendant hazards as well as its pleasures a subject of inexhaustible interest. From their writings we learn that the most dangerous roads for travellers were those that converged on London, and of these four in particular stand out. Of the four, Hounslow Heath seems to have attracted the most attention from highwaymen, or 'Knights of the High Toby' as they were often called. The great wen of Heathrow Airport has now largely covered the area concerned but in earlier times it constituted a wild tract of country on London's outer margin through which the important highway westwards to Bath and Bristol passed. Mention of the activities of highwaymen on Hounslow Heath goes back to at least 1552 and provides a good example of a robber being outwitted by his intended victim. A highwayman stopped a tailor jogging along on a somewhat winded old nag. Thinking that he had found easy game, he told the tailor to hand over all valuables on his person. The tailor agreed to do so but asked if he could take his hat off and hold it up while the robber peppered it with shot from his pistols. The tailor explained that he did not want his friends to ridicule him for being robbed without putting up any kind of a fight. The riddled hat would prove what a doughty fighter he was. The highwayman, who was clearly extremely gullible, then blazed away, emptying his pistols and turning the hat into a very fair imitation of a sieve. The tailor, who proved to be less of a hick than he looked, then produced a firearm of his own!

Second only to Hounslow Heath were two hazardous spots on the London to Dover road, Shooter's Hill and Gad's Hill. One fine moonlit night in the early eighteenth century, three notorious highwaymen named Will Ogden, Tom Reynolds and Jack Bradshaw were lurking among the trees at Shooter's Hill while commanding an unobstructed view of the road in both directions. Not one single traveller put in an appearance as the hours ticked slowly by.

Eventually, a single pedestrian came into sight, a servant-girl by her appearance. Usually they would have let her pass but they were bored and she was carrying a box. The other two told Bradshaw to accost the girl and find out if the box contained anything worth having. Bradshaw dismounted from his horse, strode up to the girl, grabbed the box and rifled through its contents. They included a number of women's garments, a hammer and at least 15s. Disgusted with the hammer, Bradshaw cast it to one side and continued to root about in the box. In a flash the girl picked the hammer up and dealt him a cracking blow on the forehead. When he fell to the ground she manoeuvred the hammer round in her hand and with the claw proceeded to rip his throat open. As Bradshaw lay expiring on the ground, a gentleman rode up and asked if he could be of assistance and suggested that he might as well go through the man's pockets. This produced only a little loose change and a whistle. The stranger raised the whistle to his lips and extracted a few notes. Ogden and Reynolds had retired to a spinney a small distance away and had not seen the worsting of their colleague at the hands of this formidable serving wench. The sound of the whistle was the agreed call for help and they rushed headlong to assist Bradshaw and seeing their mutilated colleague clearly expiring, they kept on galloping. The identity of the girl was never ascertained.

The third location infested by highway robbers was Finchley Common on the Great North Road. This place will forever be associated with Dick Turpin, of whom more later. It remained a place to be avoided long after Turpin had been hanged. For example, in 1790, the Earl of Minto coming south to London, wrote to his wife that when he arrived near Finchley, instead of proceeding on to the city that night, he would put up at an inn. He was not prepared to put the place's sinister night-time reputation to the test. There is a story that a little-known highwayman called Curtis buried a collection of booty, then valued at £1,500, on the common. Apparently he never had the opportunity to recover it and rumour says that it is still there.

Shotover Hill, close to Oxford on the road to London, was another spot favoured by highwaymen. John Cottington's resourcefulness in holding up and robbing the Army payroll wagon at this point is mentioned elsewhere. On another occasion pickings must have been meagre because a highwayman with nothing better to do stopped a dishevelled foot traveller who turned out to be a barber claiming to be down on his luck. He produced a purse that was clearly empty. The highwayman was unimpressed and was about to let the wretched man go when he decided to make use of his professional expertise and have a shave. Many would question the wisdom of demanding a shave with a cut-throat razor from a man you have just tried to rob. The barber was extremely nervous and quivered so much that he dropped his shaving pot on to a stone whereupon it shattered into smithereens. Among the fragments were twenty golden guineas. It was a good day for the highwayman after all!

Other places much frequented by highwaymen were Wimbledon Common, Barnes Common, Blackheath, and further away from London, Bagshot Heath. Salisbury Plain also had a sinister reputation. Favoured spots were those where coaches, wagons and other conveyances had to ascend hills which meant that they were travelling even more slowly than usual. As late as the mid-eighteenth century, highwaymen were still holding up travellers at locations as close to the centre of London as the Strand and St Paul's. Fashionable parts of the Metropolis offered no safe haven from highwaymen and as late as the 1780s robberies occurred in districts like Knightsbridge and Kensington, sometimes in broad daylight. Rich pickings could be had at the right time of the year on the roads into and out of the fashionable spas such as Bath and Tunbridge Wells and also the venues of prestigious sporting events, including Newmarket in Suffolk. This was famous for its horseracing and gambling which attracted the patronage of the more rakish and disreputable elements of fashionable society.

Associated with the highwaymen's haunts were the inns catering for road travellers. Many were used as safe havens by highwaymen and as sources of the information about who was on the road, who was carrying worthwhile amounts of cash and valuables and who was likely to put up an effective fight. The landlords of these establishments sometimes colluded with the highwaymen, taking a share of the proceeds without the unpleasantness of having to go out at all hours and in all weathers. Examples of these inns were the White Swan at Whitechapel and the Saracen's Head at Aldgate, both in the City of London, the Green Man at Putney Heath and the George at Woolwich.

What could the traveller do to prevent highway robbery? Travellers on horseback and by private carriage were likely to be at least moderately well off and they might travel with armed retainers. Stagecoach owners came to employ guards but the cost had to be borne by the travellers in the fares they paid. Some coach travellers carried pistols such as Queen Anne flintlocks, but the sight of these often provoked a normally non-violent robber to start getting nasty. One clever ploy used by those carrying large numbers of banknotes was to cut them in half and send one half by a later coach while carrying the other half with them. The two pieces could be reunited later. Some carried a few coins in their pockets and hoped by surrendering these to divert the attention of a robber away from more valuable items hidden away. This was risky because short-tempered highwaymen took great exception to any victims they thought were being less than co-operative. Foot-warmers were metal or earthenware bottles filled with hot water and used to provide some comfort on cold journeys. When not in use they were often housed in decorated wooden boxes and a lady traveller might secrete a small firearm in one of these.

Another trick was for the traveller to fill his purse with counterfeit money. Clearly any robber who discovered such a ploy was unlikely to let it pass by. In 1793 a Mr Burdon, travelling from London to Durham on banking business, was stopped by a highwayman and forced to surrender the 25 guineas in his purse. The robber must have thought that it was his lucky day to pick up so much easy money. On the contrary, Burdon knew that it was *his* lucky day. Hidden under the seat of his postchaise was the sum of 25,000 guineas! This may be a record for the amount unknowingly left behind by a highwayman.

Not all travellers submitted quietly to their attackers. Sometimes travellers engaged in shoot-outs with highwaymen. One gloomy November evening in 1774, Lord Berkeley was travelling in his carriage across Hounslow Heath when it was stopped by three armed riders. One of them thrust a pistol through the window, which Berkeley promptly seized and pushed aside, firing his own weapon at point-blank range. The luckless highwayman moved a few yards away and then fell off his horse, dead. His accomplices fled instantly. Seventy years earlier in 1701 Tim Buckley's career as a highwayman was brought to a dramatic and abrupt end. He held up a stagecoach near Nottingham and had his horse shot from under him. Undaunted and on foot, he let loose with each of his eight pistols in succession and managed to kill two of his opponents before sheer weight of numbers and his injuries proved too much. He was just twenty-nine.

Some highwaymen lacked the courage of their convictions, however. The Stourbridge coach was held up in 1764 by what seems to have been a particularly squeamish highwayman. He shot the guard through the head and was so appalled by what he had done that he rode off in haste without bothering to rob the passengers. Occasionally victims were able to wreak revenge on their attackers, but not always in conventional ways, as happened at Ripley in 1742. Two highwaymen stopped a lone traveller on the road near Ripley in Surrey but let him go unscathed. Elated by his lucky escape but outraged at their audacity, the traveller rode into Ripley and raised the alarm. A posse was quickly assembled which found the highwaymen and chased them on to the village green where a cricket match was taking place. They were assailed by the players with a flurry of bats and stumps. One robber escaped, but the other, having been knocked off his horse, managed to shoot a player fatally before himself being overpowered.

These episodes highlight the enormous risks that highwaymen took. Especially in the dark, unless armed with prior knowledge, they had no real idea of the sex, age or potential fighting mettle of the occupants of a coach or carriage. When thrusting their heads through the open window they might be assailed by hysterical screams, pitiful pleas for mercy or a deadly hail of bullets. They had to be brave to take such risks, but they also needed luck.

Not only live highwaymen could be found by the King's highway but dead ones too. The barbaric practice of gibbeting was reserved for the very worst scoundrels and was both punishment and execution. In the seventeenth and eighteenth centuries people were greatly concerned to be laid to rest with dignity which is exactly why this punishment was so dreaded. Strangely, gibbeting only received parliamentary sanction in 1752 for those guilty of robbing the Royal Mail, but it had been widely practised before that time. Indeed, it is first mentioned in the reign of King Henry III who ruled from 1216 to 1272. The gibbet was supposed to be a deterrent. Gibbets with their grisly human remains were located in conspicuous public places, either out in the countryside at such locations as crossroads or placed on the walls of towns, usually near gateways. In 1791 William Lewin had been hanged at Chester for robbing the mails and his body was gibbeted on Helsby Tor, a prominent bluff on which it could probably have been seen with a telescope from three counties other than Cheshire itself.

Gibbets were eye-catching and they drew crowds of the sort of people who enjoy revelling in the misfortunes of others. To preserve them, the bodies were sometimes immersed in tar and then the eyes removed. These corpses would then gaze out into space as mute sermons on the foolishness of criminal activity. Although many of those who suffered the indignity of being gibbeted may have been villains without any redeeming features, their relations often tried to take down their remains to ensure they were given a decent burial. Without this, the souls were thought to be condemned to wander forever. The simplest way of securing the body was to saw down the gibbet-pole but the authorities got wise to this trick and started encasing the poles in iron. The alternative involved shinning up the pole, no mission for the faint-hearted. The act of trying to take the corpse away, daunting in itself, became a capital offence. However, despite understandable aversion to this kind of nocturnal activity and the use by the authorities of ranks of sharp spikes placed at intervals on the gibbet-poles, the contents of the cages at the top somehow continued to be removed. As the *Annual Register* of 3 April 1763 gloomily commented, 'All the gibbets on the Edgware Road, on which many malefactors hung in chains, were cut down by persons unknown.'

On one occasion in Derbyshire the friends of the deceased hit on the idea of burning the gibbet-pole down. In this case the gibbet held three highwaymen who were known to have worked together. However, it ignited with far more gusto than had been expected and was soon blazing away out of control. Located on a hilltop, it acted like a beacon, the tar, flames and strong winds combining to create a sight that could be seen for miles. What had been intended as a rescue attempt on the mortal remains turned into a wake following a cremation. At first light, only the links of the iron chains, which had held the bodies, remained. Occasionally, convicted murderers would be hanged alive in chains, which is what happened to John Whitfield. He was apparently a highwayman of the most egregious character and was placed, while still breathing, in a gibbet on a prominent hill just south of Carlisle. He hung there for several days, shrieking in pain and desperation until by a strange irony a good Samaritan in the form of a mail coachman passed by and humanely decided to end his suffering by simply shooting him. The last person to be gibbeted was George Cook, who met his end near Leicester in 1832. The practice was abolished in 1834.

Among the lesser known highwaymen of the seventeenth century was Francis Jackson. As a highway robber he cut a poor figure, having a short and undistinguished career and being hanged at Hampstead in 1674. However, he unwittingly made a valuable contribution to history by writing an autobiography, which provides an interesting and detailed insight into the everyday actualities of highway robbery. It contains material intended to warn the traveller how to recognise a highwayman and it provides a wealth of material for the aspiring highwayman. It explains that an effective intelligence system was vital for success and that time spent watching and listening in the parlours of wayside inns and employing reliable spies in such places was the best way to acquire information about which travellers to go after and which to leave well alone. His book contains a somewhat unprincipled attack on his former colleagues as a bunch of ne'er-do-wells and wastrels, and he indignantly states that under the guise of being gentlemen highwaymen often claim for themselves titles, especially military ones, to which they have no right. However, he also explains how highwaymen should make emotional appeals for clemency in the unhappy event of being taken to court and the ways to use disguise to reduce the likelihood of detection. He even includes hints on masking the voice and suggests that in a gang of robbers only nicknames should be used so that real names cannot be extracted under duress by the authorities.

Despite the glamorous image bestowed on highwaymen, their careers were frequently short and inglorious. Tim Buckley from Stamford in Lincolnshire drifted to London, got into bad company and turned to house-breaking. With a price on his head he left London in 1701, robbed a house at Ashby-de-la-Zouch and bought a horse at Derby with the proceeds. He then went out and unwisely stopped a coach containing three gentlemen accompanied by two riders. He killed one of them before receiving eleven bullet wounds and being overpowered. A few days later his body was hanging in chains at the scene, a few miles outside Nottingham. Highwayman needed courage, experience and luck. The careers of many, however, would have been no more auspicious than Buckley's.

In spite of the threat posed by highwaymen and other robbers on the road and in the urban streets and alleys, it is evident that in the seventeenth century there were people, although few in number, who were prepared to travel for pleasure, intent on passing on their experiences to a wider public. Such a traveller was Fynes Moryson. He was intelligent and perceptive and his writings provide interesting information about the various regional dishes that a long-distance traveller might encounter as he journeyed around the British Isles at that time. Moryson regales his readers with mention of inns where a selection from such delights as woodcock, duck, snipe, plover, pigeon, partridge, great bustard, hare, boar, peacock and venison could be found to tempt the most jaded of palates. As far as fish are concerned, Moryson describes menus containing lampreys, elvers, sturgeon, pike, chub and carp. Fruits on offer included medlars, quinces, mulberries, nuts and various fungi. He seems to have been particularly fascinated by regional dishes and makes mention of Cambridge brawn, Kentish huffkins (a kind of muffin), Somerset laver (an edible seaweed), Banbury cheese and the Cornish pasty, among others. He marvels that a traveller probably had to go no further than 50 miles from his home to find that he was surrounded by different customs, different types of building and building materials, different clothes, unfamiliar items of diet and accents and dialects that might be almost incomprehensible.

As well as the occasional traveller like Moryson who was on the road for his own enjoyment, there were carriers who led a horse and small cart. They delivered a range of smallish consignments on a local basis as well as letters, verbal messages and the latest news, but were not to be confused with waggoners who drove stage-waggons. These transported much larger loads that were usually for more distant destinations, and also carried passengers when there was space available. Those who travelled by this means did so because they could afford nothing better and they would pay about a halfpenny per mile in return for which they proceeded at about 2 miles per hour. Some ballads and popular songs from the seventeenth and eighteenth centuries make much of the character of the 'jolly waggoner', which was meant as a joke because waggoners were known to be saturnine individuals.

Highwaymen obviously favoured robbing wealthy travellers wherever possible. Currency in the form of coinage was the ideal plunder because it did not require the services of a receiver. However, gold and silver items such as watches, pieces of jewellery and anything made from expensive cloth such as silk were all eagerly snapped up because they were light and easy to carry. Sometimes they seized items of baggage but these could be bulky, difficult to handle and might not contain anything worth stealing. Cheques and bills of exchange were taken once an effective banking system had been established in Britain, which did not occur until the end of the eighteenth century. However, redeeming these for cash was potentially dangerous because the robber's description would be circulated and the transaction could only be negotiated personally.

Postboys on horseback were worthwhile victims of robbery. They represented the most common means of transporting the mail until the late eighteenth century, and because they travelled alone and were unarmed they were particularly vulnerable to attack. The General Post Office offered extremely generous rewards for information leading to the arrest and conviction of those who held up postboys. The first recorded hold-up of the mails was in 1650 when a gang of highwaymen apparently stole a letter containing the sum of 11*d* from a stagewagon on Hampstead Heath. Thomas Lympus was an ex-postboy turned highwayman who himself robbed a postboy outside Reading in 1721. The Postmaster General offered a reward of £200 in addition to the normal reward for the arrest of a highwayman. Lympus escaped to France and claimed immunity from extradition by converting to Roman Catholicism. He later returned clandestinely to England and robbed another postboy between Sherborne and Crewkerne in the West Country, but this time he was caught and there was no escape.

In the seventeenth century the first stagecoach took to the road but there is doubt about the exact date. Contemporary accounts explain that in the mid-1660s there were coaches running from Holborn in London. They served such places as Exeter, a distance of 170 miles that took eight days, and York a distance of 196 miles that also took eight days. They ran only in what could be loosely described as the 'summer months', being taken off in early November and not reappearing until the end of March. These early coaches lumbered along at very slow speeds and better-off travellers preferred to move more quickly and flexibly on horseback or in their own horse-drawn conveyances. By the end of the 1680s many coach routes were operating throughout the year. However, not all travellers welcomed the development of the stagecoach system. In the first decade of the eighteenth century a certain John Cresset issued a pamphlet calling for the suppression of the stagecoaches. It is clear that he has nothing good to say about them:

> What advantage is it to men's health to be called out of their beds into their coaches an hour before day in the morning, to be hurried in them from place to place till one, two or three hours after dark, inasmuch that sitting all in the summer-time stifled with heat and choked with dust, or in the winter-time starving or freezing with the cold, or choked with filthy fogs? They are often brought to their inns by torchlight, when it is too late to sit up to get a supper, and next morning they are forced into a coach so early that they can get no breakfast . . . is it for a man's health to travel with tired jades, to be laid fast in foul ways, and forced to to wade up to the knees in mire; afterwards to sit in the cold till teams of horses can be sent to pull the coach out? . . . Is it for a man's pleasure, or advantageous to their healths or business to travel with a mixt company that he knows not how to converse with; to be affronted by the rudeness of a surly, dogged, cursing, ill-natured coachman; necessitated to lodge or bait at the worst inns on the road, where there is no accommodation fit for a gentleman; and this merely because the owners of the inns and the coachmen are agreed together to cheat the guests?

The writer of this jaundiced tirade omits even to mention the menacing threat of robbery. However, the industrious diarist John Evelyn (1620–1706) was robbed on the highroad and he duly noted the fact in his diary. Two footpads apprehended him near Bromley in Kent. They caught hold of his horse, snatched the reins from his hands, pulled him off, took his sword and dragged him into a thicket nearby where they rifled through his pockets and his baggage. They then took off his riding boots and tied him to a tree along with his horse, which had such distinctive markings that they did not dare to steal it. The robbers disappeared and for two hours Evelyn had to endure exposure to the sun and the unwanted attentions of flies and ants until he eventually managed to struggle free. He learned from this experience and a later diary entry recorded how he travelled from London to Dover with an ambassador's party. Mindful of his previous unpleasant experience near Bromley, Evelyn armed himself with a basket-hilt sword, a blunderbuss, a Turkish scimitar, a bag of bullets and a horn of gunpowder. The party encountered no robbers.

Most hold-ups occurred during daylight hours because this made it easier for an individual or gang of highwaymen to keep an eye on the coach, its occupants and the road. However, it also increased the chance of identification. Perhaps the ideal conditions were those to be found on a mild night with a lot of moonlight. Open country was favoured but in the event of a chase this might mean a long ride to find a suitable refuge. It explains why many highwaymen preferred to haunt the outskirts of towns, especially London. As late as 1715 there was still open countryside between Westminster and Kensington to the west of London and there were many occasions on which travellers were robbed in this vicinity.

In the second half of the seventeenth century, as a result of the ever-increasing flow of road traffic, the first of what came to be known as turnpike roads was established. This was on a stretch of the Great North Road that passed through Hertfordshire, Cambridgeshire and Huntingdonshire. At first travellers had to pay a tollkeeper but because there was no physical barrier to access some travellers would simply dash past the attendant without paying. For that reason, in 1695 authority was given for the erection of turnpikes. These consisted of a barrier of pikes fastened to a frame, which stretched across the road. When the traveller had paid his toll, the frame could be turned on a central pivot, clearing the way. In the eighteenth century the actual turnpikes began to be replaced by tollgates but the name was retained.

The invention of the turnpike gate and of the turnpike road itself was a significant step in the process of modernising the road system to enable it better to serve the needs of an industrialising nation. It was just one of a host of inter-related factors that came together over a period of about one-hundred years and were to render life very difficult for the 'gentlemen of the road'. Before that happened, however, highwaymen were to enjoy their glory days.

SEVEN

Highwaymen After the Restoration of the Monarchy

With the Restoration of 1660 the ranks of the highwaymen thinned out. Many of those families who supported the King, thereby suffering the sequestration of their land, now had their property restored and were unlikely to use robbery to make a political statement. The highwaymen that remained on the road were there for strictly business reasons and were professionals. Now the timid traveller made a will and commended himself to the Almighty before setting off on a journey by road. This period has bequeathed the enduring image of the gentleman mounted on a fine horse, with riding boots and spurs, cape, tricorn hat and black mask concealing the upper face. The scene is completed with a moonlit night and a lonely road. Pistol at the ready, he draws out of the shadows and orders the carriage or traveller to stop with the immortal words, 'Stand and deliver!' He is polite but firm and once convinced that he has received all the valuables that could be surrendered, he raises his hat to the ladies, perhaps shakes the gentlemen's hands and with a courtly gesture bids them adieu and gallops off across the heath. Such is the image of the 'gentleman of the road' and although it has been enormously embellished to enable novelists to sell more books and film-makers to enjoy box-office success, it contains elements of truth.

Other countries in Europe had highwaymen but nowhere else do they seem to have flourished to the same degree. Most of all on the main roads into London, but elsewhere across Britain highwaymen and footpads were to be found exacting their unofficial toll from the travelling public. They sometimes operated brazenly on the streets of London itself. There is a well-known tale of King George I, strolling one evening in his garden at Kensington, being confronted by an intruder described as a highwayman who, after climbing over the high wall, relieved the bemused monarch of his purse and watch. This unpopular King knew little English but he quickly got the robber's drift. The throne of Britain was extremely desirable for dynastic reasons but George hated the country and its people and was constantly dreaming wistfully of his palace and possessions in Hanover. He found some solace with his mistresses, who were usually remarkably fat or extremely thin, and with eating, for he was a gourmand of extraordinary capacity. The episode in the garden at Kensington must have further convinced the King that Britain was a barbaric, God-forsaken place. Accounts of the incident always insist that the robber was a highwayman, but by virtue of climbing the wall and entering the royal garden on foot he doubled as a footpad and burglar.

One reason why highway robbery was so prevalent in this country was because Britain was one of the few countries in Europe without a professional police force. Elsewhere in Europe there were military patrols to keep the roads clear and apprehend wrongdoers. In this country the Englishman was said greatly to value his freedoms, although in retrospect it is hard to ascertain what these actually were, and to think that these would be threatened by the existence of police forces. Another issue was expense – nobody wanted to pay for policing. The Highwayman Act of 1692, however, established a reward of £40 'blood money' for the capture and successful prosecution of a highway robber. This meant that the highwayman's greatest danger now lay with bounty hunters and informers. However, the English had a remarkable live-and-let-live attitude towards highwaymen and when they spoke of them to foreigners it was in the awed tones that indicated real patriotic pride. The

Abbé de Blanc, who travelled extensively in this country in the late 1730s, said that highwaymen, at least those of the gentlemanly sort, were popularly regarded as heroes and were boasted of as having more pluck than the country's regular soldiers.

Some of the highwaymen on Britain's roads in the heyday of highway robbery were gentlemen who simply lived beyond their means, such as Captain Dick Dudley. Too young to have taken part in the hostilities of the Civil War, his father, a well-to-do Northamptonshire landowner, secured a commission for his son in the Army upon the Restoration of Charles II. Dudley proved to be a strict, even draconian disciplinarian. It is alleged that while inspecting a troop of soldiers he ordered his sergeant to strike a trooper who was slightly out of line. The sergeant obeyed but the good captain thought he was insufficiently forceful. To show what he had meant Dudley then grabbed hold of the sergeant's halberd and brought it down on the unfortunate trooper's head, cleaving it in two. This episode meant that Dudley was forced to quit the Army. Finding little demand for his talents in the world of employment, he decided to put his skill with weapons and his horsemanship to good effect.

If the stories told about Dudley have any truth, he was not simply a heartless brute despite his skill with the halberd. Apparently, he had a most generous streak in him because he took great pleasure in robbing the very rich and equal pleasure in disbursing his booty to those people he felt deserved his support. However, credulity is stretched by the story that he and his men once held up a clergyman who they ordered to preach them a sermon on the wickedness of stealing. So overwhelmed were Dudley and his men by the cleric's warnings about the fate awaiting those who flouted the Eighth Commandment that they gave three cheers, restored his purse complete with its contents and had a whip-round and presented the bemused priest with the sum of 4s. On one occasion Dudley accosted a traveller who said he was a magistrate, the kind of person for whom he had a natural antipathy. The man was not lacking in personal courage and he shot Dudley's horse from under him before being wounded in the arm. Dudley accused the JP of killing his horse and commandeered the magistrate's mount for his own. However, Dudley told him that a man in his position should not have to walk home and therefore he would arrange for one ass to carry another. Dudley evidently held the law in deep contempt for he purloined a donkey from a nearby field and ordered the magistrate to mount it. He tied his victim's feet together under the animal's belly but placed him facing the beast's posterior. He whipped the donkey, which set off at a brisk trot, revelling in its new found freedom. It eventually arrived at the local county town, still carrying the magistrate, much to the delight of the local populace. It only confirmed their already deeply held belief that the law was an ass.

Dudley was a man of some quality but, unfortunately, most of those who joined the profession during the Restoration could not describe themselves as gentlemen and a variety of desperadoes were drawn towards mounted robbery on the highway. However, they must all have been people of some means because even if they managed to steal a horse, it was costly to maintain one. The lifting of the dead hand of austerity at the Restoration of the monarchy enabled the wealthy once more to flaunt the fact that they could buy the best of everything. A developing sense of economic security was accompanied by a rise in business and commercial activity, which in turn meant that more traffic was moving along the nation's roads. Prospects for highwaymen increased proportionately. The Restoration marks the start of the golden age of the highwayman, an age that was to last for not much more than 150 years.

Stories exist about chivalrous, charming robbers who apologised for intruding on travellers' time. Also, supposedly, there were affable, kind-hearted highwaymen who collected up all the valuables from a party of travellers and then handed back the small change so as not to inconvenience anyone who needed to pay for food and drink on the rest of the journey. William Hawke, who was only twenty-four when he was hanged, declared that he had been shot at many times by the victims of his robberies but that he had never returned fire. However, highway robbery was the forcible expropriation of other people's property, and no amount of self-effacing modesty and politeness from handsome, debonair gentlemen on horseback could make being robbed anything other than an unpleasant, traumatic experience.

Much more typical of the highwayman fraternity was Thomas Wilmot, executed in 1670, whose brutish ferocity led him simply to hack off the finger of a rich lady coach traveller when he found he could not remove her diamond ring in any other way. A robber on the road was in a high state of excitement and tension when accosting his victims and they sometimes had a rush of blood which caused them to abuse or even rape the female travellers. Highwaymen did not necessarily speak politely to their victims. Phrases like, 'You suffocated dogs-in-doublets and sodomitical sons of bitches – hand over your cash!' or 'you double poxed, long-arsed salivating bitch in grain!' were intended to elicit a swift and submissive reponse to the highwayman's request.

One particularly notorious gang led by the brutal Richard Bracy was active in the East Midlands in the 1670s. Their favourite locations were Derby, Newark and Nottingham. Bracy was an extremely dangerous man, who had a violent temper and seemed to enjoy beating and torturing his victims. At the age of seventeen he is said to have bludgeoned a young girl to death. Certainly the gang's activities were marked by gratuitous violence and they completely lacked the decorum and courtesy with which many highwaymen have been associated. On one occasion they were sitting in an inn making their plans when they realised that they had been overheard by the young pot-boy. They seized and murdered him. Bracy's luck ran out when he was apprehended in bed with his wife, who ran an inn. He spent little time with her but occasionally resorted to the inn when he felt it was wise to lie low for a while. One of the servants informed the authorities that Bracy was at the inn and he was taken without a struggle. It is not known whether Bracy dominated his gang through fear or because of his natural talents at leadership, but once he had been executed the other members were quickly apprehended and called to account. Unlike many highwaymen who were regarded as popular heroes, there were no cheers and no flowers offered up when these men went to meet the hangman.

Some highwaymen gained a fearsome reputation for gratuitous violence. They assaulted their victims and shot or hamstrung their horses to delay pursuit. One anonymous highwayman waylaid a lone traveller and was so incensed when he found that he was carrying less than a pound that he beat him up, stripped him and, according to some accounts, nailed him by his foreskin to a tree. Patrick Fleming was alleged to have cut off the nose, lips and ears of a man foolish enough to have refused to co-operate. Andrew Baynes made a habit of taking his victims' clothes and leaving them totally naked if they had no money or valuables, but not before giving them an awful thrashing with his riding crop. Patrick O'Bryan, who had deserted from the Coldstream Guards, murdered an obstinate traveller and hacked him to pieces with his sword. On a later occasion, accompanied by his gang of evil ruffians, he broke into a house in Wiltshire and brutally raped the daughter of the family, then stabbed her, took away about £2,500 and set fire to the house. The house was entirely destroyed and the servants who had been tied up by the gang all perished in the flames. A Scottish highwayman named Gilders Roy was so incensed when he stopped a judge who resisted parting with his valuables that his gang stripped his two footmen, tied them up and threw them into a pond, whereupon they drowned. Roy himself smashed the judge's carriage, shot the horses and then hanged his hapless victim. However, a Nottinghamshire physician was spared by a highwayman who recognised him and said that he could not rob the man who had saved his mother's life, kept her in food when she was ill and never charged her a penny.

Highwaymen did not curb their violent ways when they came across female travellers, but some women were not the sort to be browbeaten easily. One such was the Duchess of Mazarin, a courtesan of outstanding beauty who was prominent during the reign of Charles II. She was held up by James Collet who must rank among the more unusual highwayman in that his working clothes were the full robes of a bishop, one of his earlier victims. The Duchess, by no means put out when confronted by an apparently episcopal brigand, admitted to having 100 guineas in her possession, but being sure that the prelate was a fair-minded man, suggested a game of dice to decide whether or not she should surrender her money. It so happened that Collet had a pair of dice. They threw the dice again and again and not only did the Duchess safeguard her riches, but literally won everything that Collet had on him. Sadder and wiser, Collet, as he wandered off presumably naked, must have pondered long and hard over the powers of the gentle sex. He did not stay down in the dumps for very long and a few days later he held up the Bishop of Winchester and was therefore able to equip himself with a new disguise.

Not all highwaymen operating on England's roads in the seventeenth century were of English origin. It might easily be assumed that a foppish fellow calling himself Claude Duval was a poseur operating under an alias, but this was not so. It appears that Duval was born in Normandy in 1643 and that was his real name. He was not highborn – his father was a miller and his mother was the daughter of a humble tailor. As a youth he drifted to Paris, where he made friends with several English Royalist exiles who were eagerly waiting for the monarchy to be restored. When Charles II ascended the throne, Duval emigrated to England, where it did not occur to him to seek honest employment. There was a general sense of relief at the end of the Puritan stranglehold and a wish among the majority of the population to return to the good old days. In this situation the rich put on their finery once more and took to the roads, travelling between their estates, on business or visiting friends and relations. The resulting increase in road traffic drew the attention of the criminal underworld and precipitated a boom in highway robbery.

Duval quickly found his natural forte and became the most wanted miscreant in the columns of the *London Gazette*, which regularly published the descriptions of the most wanted criminals and the rewards offered for their apprehension. Duval also became well known for the polished courtesy with which he carried out his robberies and for his Gallic good looks, of which he made great use when flirting with the coy damsels and tremulous maidens he encountered. All over the country women travellers started their journeys harbouring hopes that this French cavalier might waylay them. Duval is credited with a host of conquests, ranging from thirteen-year-old virgins to women of extremely advanced years. Some accounts, however, say that he was not so much amorous as solicitous towards the female sex and that he never allowed salacious thoughts to besmirch the honourable and respectful way in which he conducted himself with all women, even those he was robbing.

The most famous of Duval's exploits was the occasion on which he is said to have danced a coranto with a wealthy and winsome lady who was one of the occupants of a carriage that Duval stopped on Hounslow Heath. When the highwaymen stopped the coach, the lady, to show that she was unafraid, produced a few notes on a flageolet or small flute. Entranced by this unexpected response, Duval, who by coincidence also happened to have a flageolet on his person, then entertained the assembled company with a few tunes of his own. Presumably one of Duval's colleagues then took over on the flageolet because Duval and the lady proceeded to treat the spectators to a virtuoso performance of the dance known as the coranto, a feat made all the more remarkable because Duval was wearing a pair of very substantial French riding boots. Duval is supposed to have asked the woman's husband for the full £400 he was carrying as payment for the entertainment to which he had just been treated. The story goes that Duval was offered just £100 and that he accepted this sum without demur. This calls into question the veracity of the whole episode. After all, Duval was leader of a gang

Robin Hood, the 'People's Hero'. The legends that developed around Robin Hood's activities gave rise to the idea of the 'gentleman-robber', which was then perpetuated in the stories that circulated about highwaymen. In reality most highway robbers were violent and out for quick gain.

The successful seventeenth-century highwayman James Hind robbing Colonel Harrison in Maidenhead Thicket.

The notorious pickpocket and highway robber 'Moll Cutpurse'.

William Davis, also known as the 'Golden Farmer', robs a tinker at gunpoint.

'Old Mob' robbing Judge Jeffreys. It must have given 'Old Mob' enormous satisfaction to make the hated Judge Jeffreys one of his victims. Jeffreys was notorious for taking a sadistic delight in imposing the most ferocious penalties on offenders that the law would allow. In robbing him 'Old Mob' would have been cast in the role of popular hero.

SIXTEEN STRING JACK
Pubd Oct. 6 1774

Jack Rann, the diminutive dandified highwayman known as 'Sixteen String Jack' because of the eight tags he wore at each knee.

of men who, like him, had taken to the road because they lacked the skills or the inclination to earn a living by honest means. He would not have retained his dominant position for long if he had constantly put chivalry and generosity before the need to reward his followers in cash or kind, the only language that they would have understood.

Accounts of incidents often became distorted, as can be illustrated by a story involving Duval and his gang holding up a coach on Blackheath to the south-east of London. The coach contained several ladies, one of whom was feeding a baby with a silver feeding bottle. There are two very conflicting accounts of what happened next. One says that Duval greedily seized the bottle and was just about to pocket it when one of the gang reminded him of his reputation of civility and gentleness towards women. With reluctance Duval then handed the bottle back. The other account, not wanting to show Duval in any kind of unfavourable light, says that it was Duval who remonstrated with a member of the gang who had snatched the bottle and then persuaded him to return it.

Much of the biographical detail we have about Duval comes from the pen of a contemporary writer, Dr William Pope, who published *The Memoirs of Monsieur Du Vall* (sic) in 1670, shortly after Duval's execution. Pope, a professor of anatomy at Oxford, seems to have been more concerned to produce a good story for the reading and buying public than to confine himself simply to the facts. If he is to be believed, highway robbery was just one of Duval's many talents, which also included card-sharping and confidence tricks. For all the air of mystery and glamour that surrounded Duval, nemesis eventually overtook him in a London pub called The Hole in the Wall, where one night, stupefied with drink, he was easily overcome and arrested. Forced to stand trial, Duval was convicted and sentenced to death. It is said that numerous rich and fashionable ladies attempted to intercede on his behalf but without success and he was hanged at Tyburn on 21 January 1670, still only twenty-seven years of age. A substantial crowd turned out for his funeral. Many were probably jilted but still doting ex-lovers or fathers and husbands assuring themselves that this rapacious paramour was indeed being consigned to the grave. His body lay in state for several days in a pub near Covent Garden and was visited by numbers of veiled ladies of quality who were apparently inconsolable in their grief at his premature demise. Duval was buried in the churchyard of St Paul's, Covent Garden, and his headstone bears an epitaph that starts with the following words:

> Here lies Du Vall [*sic*]: Reader, if male thou art,
> Look to thy purse; if female to thy heart.
> Much havoc has he made of both; for all
> Men he made stand, and women he made fall.
> The second Conqueror of the Norman race,
> Knights to his arms did yield, and Ladies to his face.
> Old Tyburn's glory; England's illustrious thief,
> Du Vall, the Ladies' Joy; Du Vall, the Ladies' Grief.

Some enterprising highwaymen diversified their activities into other areas of crime and one such was John or William Nevison, otherwise known as 'Swift Nicks'. He ran a lucrative sideline extorting protection money from the drovers who herded vast quantities of livestock from the northern hill country to the lush pastures of the Home Counties, where the animals were fattened up before being slaughtered for the London market. Nevison provided an excellent service and those who made use of it knew that they would experience no attention from rustlers or other thieves while on the road. Although he found that protection rackets helped to pay the bills, Nevison's main interest lay with highway robbery.

Nevison was born in 1640 near Pontefract in the West Riding of Yorkshire, probably the son of a well-to-do wool merchant. At school he showed signs of intellectual potential, but preferred to channel his energy into leading a gang of youthful delinquents who went around causing mayhem in the Pontefract area. His activities did not endear him to the school authorities and when he was caught stealing a valuable piece of cutlery they gave him a sound thrashing in front of his peers. Mortified by this experience, he decided then and there to draw his schooldays to an end. He purloined a horse belonging to one of the schoolmasters, stole £10 from his father and rode off, fuming but free, to find out what the streets of London had to offer.

At first it seems that Nevison applied himself diligently as a clerk and indeed seems to have made such a good impression that his employer instructed him to go and collect an outstanding debt. The amount involved was £200 and Nevison was unable to resist the temptation. He absconded to the continent but returned later to make his peace with his parents. His mother had died in the meantime but he returned the £10 that he had stolen and effected a reconciliation with his father, who himself passed away soon afterwards. Nevison may have been frustrated in his hope to enjoy a sizeable legacy but he received enough to buy himself a horse and all the paraphernalia required to start out as a highwayman.

Nevison proved highly resourceful and developed a reputation as a gentleman-robber who was generous to the poor and extended every courtesy and consideration when robbing members of the female sex, apart, of course, from refraining from the actual robbery itself. Nevison's greatest claim to fame is that it was probably he who undertook the headlong ride to York, so often mistakenly ascribed to Dick Turpin. It is said that he had carried out a robbery at Gad's Hill in Kent and thought that one of his victims had recognised him. To establish an alibi that would 'prove' that he had not been anywhere near Kent at the time, he embarked on the memorable 230-mile ride to York. He travelled at an average of about 14 miles per hour. When he got there, he took part in a game of bowls, chatting to such an unimpeachable witness as the Mayor of York as he did so. He was tried for the robbery in Kent but acquitted. As he intended, the court was convinced that he could not possibly have been in York so soon after the robbery in Kent.

Nevison had attracted the attention of no less a person that Charles II who summoned him to his presence, having heard that Nevison had indiscreetly been boasting of his achievement. Aware that he could not be tried again for the same offence, Nevison described the ride in detail and said that he had ridden as fast as 'Owd Nick', the Devil, himself. The King was clearly delighted by the whole episode and promptly gave him a new title: 'Swift Nicks'.

Later, when found guilty of several other robberies and languishing in the condemned cell, Nevison offered to turn King's evidence on his associates if he was allowed to live. The authorities agreed to this but Nevison, on being reprieved, then reneged on his promise. The authorities did not know what to do next and ordered him to be detained during His Majesty's Pleasure. This was a dreary prospect and Nevison eagerly took up the option of joining the Army instead. Having done so, he immediately deserted and met up again with the associates on whom he had refused to inform. By now there was a considerable price on his head and one of the gang betrayed him for the reward. He found himself incarcerated in Leicester Gaol and, his reputation having preceded him, was under especially close guard. However, Nevison had not given up yet. His friends visited him in the condemned cell and one, claiming to be a doctor, declared that Nevison had bubonic plague. This caused the gaolers to panic, terrified at the probable effect of the plague in the already unhealthy conditions of the prison. If Nevison thought that they would immediately release him as the vector of the disease, he must have been disappointed when he was placed in solitary confinement instead. The self-appointed 'doctor' made several more visits and finally, having painted him with blue spots and dosed him with a heavy sedative, informed the prison governor that Nevison was dead. This ploy worked well and the highwayman was 'buried' the next day. By sleight-of-hand what was actually buried was a weighted coffin and Nevison soon returned to his old haunts and habits.

Nevison quickly found that as the ghost of a highwayman, especially one with the reputation of 'Swift Nicks', he was even more successful than when he had been living flesh and blood. Few travellers needed prompting when told to stand and deliver by a highwayman who everyone knew was dead and buried. Even the bolder ones thought twice before loosing off a shot at a phantom. It was an ingenious but necessarily short-lived trick as the news quickly spread that Nevison had not returned from the grave because he had never been there in the first place. Life was increasingly difficult for Nevison now because the prize offered for his capture had gone up considerably. The treacherous landlord of an inn he used regularly, tempted by the reward, spiked his drink and then sent for the authorities. Nevison took one sip, then realised what had happened and fought his way out of the inn, making sure that he killed the perfidious host as he left. Up went the reward money again. Nevison had good cause to suspect innkeepers and his luck ran out when the landlady of another of his favourite watering holes conspired with some of the regular customers to call the authorities next time he stopped by for a drink. Nevison was caught, the landlady and her regulars shared the reward and this time there was no escape. He was hanged at York in 1684 or 1685, but not before treating an appreciative crowd to a boastful and racy account of his life and adventures.

Highwaymen seem to have been proud of their profession, particularly when they bathed in the admiration of the crowds who wished them well on their way to be executed and when they arrived at the scaffold. The rewards might be great but so were the risks. Why should anyone take up such a hazardous way of life if they could find something better? There was always the chance that even an absolute beginner, with bravura and luck, might pull off a lucrative robbery. Seasoned highwaymen probably believed that just one more robbery would enable them to retire. This very rarely happened because most of them enjoyed drinking, womanising and gambling, and when the money ran out they quickly returned to robbery. The hazardous nature of the job usually meant it was a short-lived career.

Born in 1627 at Wrexham in Denbighshire, William Davis practised as a highwayman for the unusually long time of forty years. What makes him even more remarkable is that his wife and eighteen children never suspected that he was leading a double life. All his acquaintances thought of him as a hard-working farmer, which indeed he was, a good husband and father, a pillar of the Church and a known generous contributor to good causes. He was well regarded because he always paid his debts promptly and in gold coin, hence his nickname 'The Golden Farmer'. Little did they know how he got much of this gold. He farmed near Bagshot Heath in Surrey, notorious as a haunt of highwaymen and he contributed to its notoriety by waylaying travellers single-handed along the roads of the district. He did this both by night and day and was helped by a range of masterly disguises that allowed him to operate with impunity for such a long time.

William Davis had few scruples about robbing other members of the farming fraternity but one of his boldest exploits was the robbing of his own landlord. This man called on Davis to collect the annual rent and went away contentedly with the resulting 70 guineas. As soon as he had gone, Davis changed his clothes, put on a disguise and galloped across country to get ahead of the landlord. He apprehended the landlord who did not recognise him and vainly pleaded poverty. Davis recovered his rent money and some days later provided an attentive and sympathetic listener to the selfsame landlord pouring out his woes about the robbery. On another occasion he was travelling down the Oxford Road when he fell in with a lawyer who, as they jogged along together, naively revealed that he was carrying £50. It was so easy to whip out a pistol and rob the hitherto unsuspecting lawyer. As with so many tales about the activities of highwaymen, this story should be viewed with some scepticism because the theme of highwaymen duping and robbing members of the legal profession recurs frequently. It is likely that attitudes towards lawyers have not changed markedly over the centuries and that the populace revelled in the idea that the gentlemen of the road outwitted people they regarded as parasites. It was no accident that there were alehouses called The Honest Lawyer with a sign showing a figure in legal accoutrements but without a head.

'The Golden Farmer' did not enjoy a glorious end, according to the legends. He had been successful for so long because he always carefully weighed up the odds before embarking on a robbery, but perhaps old age finally took its toll. His last robbery was carried out on the Exeter coach but he made the careless mistake of failing to search for firearms. As he turned to ride away, one of the travellers in the coach shot him in the back and he fell from his horse and was easily captured. When his identity was revealed, it caused a major sensation and few who knew him could believe that the highly respected, generous, hard-working and upright farmer was actually also a highway robber. His wife and his children, grown up by this time, are supposed to have hung their heads in shame. 'The Golden Farmer' was executed in 1689 or 1690. At one time there was a public house in the locality named after him.

Contemporary with William Davis was Thomas Sympson, known as 'Old Mob'. He was based at Romsey in Hampshire but seems to have travelled far and wide and gained an enviable reputation for audacity and resourcefulness. One day, near Honiton in Devon, he encountered none other than Sir Bartholomew Shower. This wealthy knight declared that he only had small change on his person but this did not disconcert 'Old Mob' who forced Shower to draw up a money draft, payable on sight at one of the leading goldsmiths in the nearby city of Exeter. He tied the disconcerted Shower to a tree and rode off to Exeter to redeem his draft. 'Old Mob' was not totally heartless because he returned to the scene and untied his victim but, since his horse had already been turned loose, Sir Bartholomew had no alternative but to walk home.

Pedlars of cure-all medicines have existed for centuries and although their patter and their products have been a constant source of hope for some, they have widely been regarded as charlatans.

'Old Mob' was fond of delivering long-winded lectures to his victims and when he waylaid a well-known quack he told him sternly: 'You have put out more eyes than the smallpox, made more deaf than the cataracts of the Nile, lamed more than the gout, shrunk more sinews than one that makes bow-strings, and killed more than the pestilence!' Clearly, 'Old Mob' was fond of taking the moral high ground. When he apprehended the Duchess of Portsmouth, a woman of easy virtue and humble origins who had been showered with titles and possessions by a grateful monarch in appreciation of the services that she had rendered, 'Old Mob' could not resist calling her an 'outlandish whore'. He numbered the hated Judge Jeffreys among his victims and did not let him go without delivering a homily: 'I don't doubt that when justice has overtaken us both, I shall stand at least as good a chance as your lordship, who have [*sic*] already written your name in indelible characters of blood by putting to death so many hundred innocent men, for only standing up in defence of our common liberties . . .' Having delivered this harangue, 'Old Mob' proceeded to the more important business of relieving Jeffreys of the sum of 56 guineas.

On another occasion, 'Old Mob' learned that a well-to-do peer of the realm was about to travel from Bath to London. His lordship's fame was based largely on his lecherous proclivities and 'Old Mob' decided that he could take advantage of this. He disguised himself very effectively as a woman and was soon invited to join the peer and his small party of attendants. He flirted outrageously and his lordship, clearly thinking that his luck was in, made an unambiguous, even brazen suggestion to his new and alluring companion. 'Old Mob' consented on condition that they left the attendants and found a suitably secluded spot in which to consummate their mutual passion. Having accepted this, his lordship, with lust unrequited, was soon relieved of his money. 'Old Mob' enjoyed a long and varied career but one that ended on the scaffold in 1691.

Britain was involved in a number of wars in the second half of the seventeenth century, for example, with the Dutch in the 1670s and with the French in 1689 in the War of the League of Augsburg. During wartime there were inevitably many men who deserted the Army. By doing so they automatically put themselves outside the law and became fugitives. When wars ended, demobilised, brutalised men likewise found themselves without obvious lawful means of support. Deserters and demobilised men often took to crime and some became highwaymen. John Withers, a deserter, was a merciless thug who mixed working as a footpad with violent sorties on horseback. On one occasion, having had his horse shot from under him and desperate for money to buy another, he and his accomplice were on foot when they waylaid a postman in London in broad daylight. Neither Withers or his companion was masked, and so to get rid of the only witness to the robbery Withers calmly cut the poor postman's throat. They then took the body to a nearby stream after ripping it open and filling it with pebbles to weigh it down. Possibly more sadistic was William Cady, a graduate of Cambridge University, who is reputed to have held up a well-to-do merchant and his wife. He demanded an expensive-looking ring on the woman's finger, whose plea that it was of great sentimental value was wasted on the impatient and volatile Cady. He made to seize her hand but she was too quick for him and pulled off the ring, swallowing it there and then. Enraged, Cady is said to have shot her in the head, ripped her open and recovered the ring, watched with mesmerised horror by her husband. This is one of many highwaymen's tales for which there is no serious supporting evidence and while it is certain that some highway robbers were capable of appalling violence, this particular episode challenges belief.

Highway robbers on horseback and highway robbers on foot have been described but who could resist the idea of a highway robber on ice? Jonathan Simpson was one such highwayman who operated on skates! The winter of 1683–4 was exceptionally cold and few travellers were prepared to risk using the roads. Consequently, there was little business to be done by those robbers who were not prepared to alter their *modus operandi*. The River Thames in

London was firmly frozen from early December to the beginning of February. Such was the attraction of walking on the Thames that enterprising businessmen set up stalls on the ice and eventually a 'Frost Fair' extended for about a mile from the Temple to Southwark. Large crowds appeared and these also attracted people with criminal intent. Simpson equipped himself with skates and found that rich pickings were to be had by simply knocking people over on the ice, apparently by accident, and then robbing them as they floundered about in confusion attempting to regain their feet.

One of the most interesting and ingenious highwaymen of the seventeenth century was James Whitney who assumed the title 'Captain', although he had never actually been an officer in the Army. He was of humble origin and, like Dick Turpin, was apprenticed to a butcher. Also like Turpin, he found the trade boring and was dismissed, later becoming the landlord of The George at Cheshunt in Hertfordshire. Those who worked in the licensed trade had to perform a delicate balancing act. They wanted the good business that highwaymen often brought but they did not want to risk losing their licences if the magistrates thought they were providing a base for known villains. Whitney enjoyed having highwaymen in his bar with their roistering talk and devil-may-care manner. They liked him too and often suggested that he should take to the road himself. Why work so hard for little reward when just one profitable robbery could net much more than he earned in an entire year? These blandishments eventually had their effect and Whitney sold his inn, bought a handsome, strong horse and a brace of pistols and set off in search of adventure.

Whitney's first victim was a prosperous-looking clergyman. Whitney took his money and, perhaps more surprisingly, his clerical habit. A few minutes later he came across an extremely dishevelled and impoverished rural curate to whom he immediately gave some money and his first victim's smart vestments. One day Whitney was patrolling Bagshot Heath, fully disguised, when he accosted an affluent-looking rider and, whipping out his pistols, called on him to halt and deliver. The stranger's response was that he was about to do exactly the same thing. He told Whitney that he too was a highwayman. They agreed to go their separate ways. However, in the evening Whitney, still in disguise, dropped into an inn for refreshment and heard the same man holding forth about how he had outwitted a highwayman and saved the hundred pounds he was carrying by pretending to be a highwayman himself. Whitney ascertained that the man was staying at the inn and took a room himself. Next morning he watched the pseudo-highwayman trot off down the road and, wearing another disguise, followed and caught him up. The man used the same ploy again but Whitney was ready for it and must have taken great pleasure in relieving the boasting impostor of his £100. By the standards of his kind, Whitney seems to have lacked malice and shunned violence where possible, but these redeeming features were of no use when he was finally captured. He was executed either in 1693 or 1694.

Jack Bird was from Lincolnshire and, like James Whitney, had been apprenticed to a respectable trade, in this case as a baker. It bored him, so he ran away and joined the Army, deserted and then made for Holland, where he was arrested after committing a robbery. He was sentenced to hard labour something very much against his natural inclination and so the authorities placed him in chains and put him in a large tank which then started filling up with water, much to Bird's alarm. They provided him with a hand pump and told him they would be back in about an hour's time to see whether he had changed his mind about performing physical labour or had drowned. When they returned, Bird was vigorously pumping away.

Having completed his sentence, Bird made his way back to England, stole a horse and started life as a highwayman. His career on the road was fairly unexceptional until one day he held up a coach containing a somewhat quirky baron, his chaplain and two servants. Bird demanded their money and the baron offered him 20 guineas if he would fight him for it. The chaplain, however, intervened and took his master's place. It was clear that the chaplain was no mean pugilist and Bird was hard pressed but eventually he prevailed. The baron was most generous in his praise and declared that it was the first time he had seen the chaplain worsted. He handed over the 20 guineas without demur. Bird was arrested and charged with a number of robberies, found guilty and hanged in 1690.

These may have seemed good times for highwaymen. The hold of the forces of law and order was, at best, tenuous and the roads were becoming busier and busier. The temptation of quick money was too much for the men whose activities have been described. However, few cheated the hangmen and died of natural causes.

EIGHT

Some Eighteenth-century Highwaymen

'Sixteen String Jack' was born near Bath in Somerset in 1750 and christened John Rann. He was bright and quick-witted and at the age of twelve took service with a lady of sufficient means to move in the fashionable society of the time. He did well, gaining one promotion after another and became a coachman in London where, unfortunately, there were too many temptations. The capital was alive with toothsome young doxies and also contained many shops with elegant and expensive clothes. Jack developed a taste for both and took great pleasure in swaggering around at public events dressed like a fashionable grandee and making the acquaintance of the young ladies who flocked to such occasions to eye up the young bloods. The problem was that a humble coachman's pay could not finance a lifestyle of the sort to which Jack aspired. There seemed no alternative to a life of rigorous self-denial or crime – he chose the latter. He tried his hand at pickpocketing but decided that it was risky and lacked style. Jack wanted to cut a dash and so decided to turn his hand to the highwayman's trade. He proved to be a natural.

'Sixteen String Jack' soon became notorious for the audacity of his robberies and the gentlemanly courtesy with which he demanded that his victims part with their valuables. He was also noted for his sartorial elegance and gained his strange nickname because he frequently appeared in public in breeches of silk that had sixteen strings attached to the knees. He was arrested many times and charged with highway robbery but was acquitted because witnesses could not confirm his identity. Jack just could not keep out of the limelight, nor did he wish to. Once he pushed his way to the front of a crowd eagerly awaiting a hanging at Tyburn dressed in such an outrageously extroverted fashion that he almost stole the show from the condemned prisoner. He told people in the crowd that one day he would be the main participant in the proceedings at Tyburn, not merely a spectator.

On one occasion Jack was caught and charged with housebreaking. Although he considered burglary to be a menial crime way beneath him, he was caught red-handed, and to add to the ignominy he was actually arrested by one of the scorned 'Charleys' or decrepit old night-watchmen who were the butt of so much ribald humour at the time. Jack was hauled up before John Fielding, the 'Blind Beak', and related the sad story of how he had actually been making a call on a young lady, Doll Frampton. The tryst had been arranged for earlier that evening but Jack had been unavoidably delayed and Doll had given him up and retired to bed. Jack explained that he dared not knock on the door in case he awoke the other residents and so, not wishing to let Dolly down completely, he decided to break in but was caught in the act. Dolly made something of a sensation when she appeared in court to testify on Jack's behalf dressed in a low-cut bodice. Jack was an engaging fellow and the 'Blind Beak' must have been feeling unusually charitable that day because he sent him away with a warning as to his future conduct. Jack left the court, his face wreathed in smiles, but then had to go home to face the justifiable wrath of Eleanor, his long-standing mistress.

By all accounts Jack was a cheerful, well-liked man and a favourite of the ladies. This was particularly evident when his luck had finally run out and he was in the condemned cell at Newgate. There he received many visitors, predominantly female ones, and even hosted a farewell dinner just before the date set for his execution. This gregarious and extrovert character made his final journey to Tyburn in November 1774, and used the occasion of his appearance on the scaffold to exchange banter with the hangman and to quip with a highly appreciative crowd. He had never dressed more extravagantly, wearing a suit of pea-green clothes ordered specially for the occasion with a large nosegay as an accessory.

Like Jack Rann, Jerry Abershaw was another not overawed by the majesty of the law. Abershaw was born in 1773 and was only seventeen years of age when he became a member of a gang of highwaymen who operated mainly on Putney Heath and Wimbledon Common and whose headquarters were at the nearby Bald Faced Stag. Jerry seems to have been more reticent than many of his kind and very little is known about him, except that he had a career on the road that lasted five years, during which time he defied every measure taken by the Bow Street Runners to capture him. One of his partners-in-crime was Richard Ferguson whose horsemanship skills were such that he won the nickname 'Galloping Dick'. Ferguson was born in Hertfordshire and was about the same age as Abershaw. Their working relations began in unusual circumstances.

'Galloping Dick' gained employment as a postilion and made a very good impression until he was caught *in flagante delicto* with one of the female servants and was promptly dismissed. Shortly afterwards his father died, leaving him a small inheritance which allowed him to set up as a man-about-town. He took himself to the theatre in Drury Lane and found himself sitting next to a very attractive young woman. She was a prostitute of a superior sort but Dick fell madly in love with her and showered her with all manner of presents which she was only too happy to accept. His income could not match the expenses he was accruing in courting the lovely Nancy and he was forced to get work as a postilion once more.

One evening as 'Galloping Dick' drove a gentleman along the Great North Road he was stopped by two highwaymen, one of whom he recognised as another of Nancy's paramours. Abershaw realised that he had been recognised and went to an inn that Dick frequented and bribed him to keep silent. Abershaw alluded disparagingly to Dick's employment as a mere postilion, working in a servile capacity for a pittance and persuaded him to join his band. At first Dick acted as an informant identifying likely victims for robbery and only later as a fully fledged highwayman. This was shortly before Abershaw himself was caught, tried and condemned to death. Abershaw enraged the judge by mimicking him when he put the black cap on to pronounce the death sentence. He also displayed his complete contempt for authority by decorating the walls of his cell in Newgate with representations of his adventures, painted with a substance said to consist of the juice of black cherries. He was hanged on 3 August 1795 on Kennington Common and gave the crowd good value because of his nonchalance and the scorn he poured on the law and its representatives in the speech he made from the scaffold. His body was gibbeted at Putney and attracted large crowds. 'Galloping Dick' was caught and likewise hanged five years later.

William Parsons was born in 1717, the youngest son of a baronet and the nephew of the Duke of Northumberland. He could not plead poverty as a reason for taking to the road as a highwayman, and his father had always treated him well and ensured that he received a good education. Parsons is the only Old Etonian to feature in these pages as a highway robber. He was a habitual gambler and to pay the debts that were continually piling up he stole quite shamelessly from family and friends, including relieving his illustrious aunt of a gold-mounted miniature. The theft and his part in it were quickly discovered and his contrite father packed him off into the Royal Navy as a midshipman, but this new venture did not last long.

Parsons was discovered cheating at cards and this was viewed with almost the same degree of seriousness as cowardice in action or corresponding with the enemy. He was forced to leave the Navy and his father then sent him to do an administrative job in West Africa, but he still had debts to pay for which he forged a letter from his aunt purporting to guarantee him for up to £70. When the lady discovered the deception she altered her will, under which Parsons would have been the sole beneficiary. She died some time later leaving £25,000. Penniless, he returned to England and married a girl with a dowry of £4,000, but this was soon spent and he enlisted in the Army as an ensign. He could not keep out of trouble and after being found guilty of forgery was transported to Virginia. There he was noticed by the benevolent and gullible Lord Fairfax who regretted that one of Parsons' pedigree should have come down so much in the world. He did Parsons several kind services and the latter rewarded him by stealing one of his finest horses, mounted on which he went on the road as a highwayman.

Parsons met with considerable success in his new-found career and presumably acquired enough money to get the return fare home because he is next heard of in England. His aunt had just died and left her large fortune to his sister, but Parsons was determined to get his hands on it. He plotted with an accomplice, a disreputable ex-footman, who would try to woo her into marriage and, failing that, terrify her into becoming his wife but this scheme was soon discovered and had to be abandoned. The egregious Parsons returned to robbery to finance his gambling habit but was caught on Hounslow Heath and hanged at the age of thirty-four despite the efforts of his influential relations to secure him a reprieve. Nothing can be said in his favour.

A striking number of the sons of clergymen also ended up on the scaffold, often as a result of committing robbery on the highways. This may be because their fathers had social status but often lacked the income necessary to ape the lives of the rich landowners that were their patrons and with whom they mixed. The sons, therefore, got a taste of the lifestyle of the very rich and, liking what they saw, decided that they wanted some of it. The income required could not possibly be gained through honest toil and so it was natural to drift into gambling and highway robbery. One example of this is James Maclaine, whose conduct earned him the nickname 'Gentleman Highwayman' during his lifetime.

Maclaine's father was a Presbyterian minister of Scottish origins with a living in County Monaghan in Ireland. James was well educated and had been destined to enter business as a clerk. However, his father died when he was aged eighteen leaving him a sizeable inheritance. This was quickly spent and Maclaine to his chagrin had to take a job as a butler. The wages for such a job could not possibly support the lifestyle that Maclaine hankered after and so he started stealing and selling items of his employer's property. The thefts were discovered and he was discharged with a bad character. However, he moved to London where he managed to obtain further domestic employment while developing a taste for expensive women. He had charm, looks and style and soon met a woman who attracted him because of the £500 dowry she would bring the man who married her. With the £500 the couple, once married, set up a grocery business but trade was poor and when his wife died Maclaine decided to try his luck as an eligible widower in the fashionable towns of Bath and Tunbridge Wells where conquests and generous dowries might be found. He posed as a gentleman of breeding and substance and engaged a bankrupt apothecary named Plunkett to act as his 'footman' but in reality to be his partner-in-crime. Maclaine was disappointed to find that few women were falling over themselves to share his bed let alone place dowries at his disposal in exchange for matrimony. Establishing these hard facts of life proved very expensive and when Plunkett suggested that they should become highwaymen it seemed an excellent idea.

Maclaine and Plunkett did quite well from highway robbery but the credit must actually go to Plunkett, as the very idea of stopping strangers on the highway and demanding their valuables distressed Maclaine. He was a congenital coward who hated the idea of waving pistols around or any other physical unpleasantness. Therefore, he always allowed Plunkett to take the lead whenever personal courage was required while he continued avidly to pursue ladies. On two or three occasions he almost secured unions supported by a substantial dowry, but each time the lady concerned called the nuptials off at the last moment. Maclaine nearly married the sister of the Duke of Newcastle, the Prime Minister. The wooing of such ladies was an extremely expensive business and Maclaine had to take suitably prestigious accommodation in London's West End. To look the part, he started wearing a crimson damask frock coat, a silk waistcoat with lace trimmings and black velvet breeches, white silk stockings and yellow morocco slippers.

Plunkett with Maclaine cowering timorously nearby had many rewarding successes on the road, the best-known of which was their hold-up of Horace Walpole (1717–97), the well-known author who recorded the experience in his writings. It happened in Hyde Park one moonlit night in 1749 and Walpole does not disclose how much he was actually forced to hand over. He does mention, however, that he was shot at by Maclaine and that Maclaine's pistol, 'going off accidentally, razed the skin under my eye, left some marks of shot on my face, and stunned me. The ball went through the top of the chariot, and, if I had sat an inch nearer to the left side, must have gone through my head.' Apparently, the following morning he received a very polite, cultured letter from Maclaine offering his apologies for any inconvenience caused. Walpole's comment was that his brief relationship with the highwayman was carried out 'with the greatest good breeding on both sides'.

Money, or rather the lack of it, continued to be the bane of life for this rather ill-assorted duo and it probably spurred them on to commit two robberies in one night. The first was to hold up the Salisbury stagecoach at Turnham Green, just west of London, where they carried away a case containing clothes belonging to a Mr Higden. Later, at Hounslow Heath they held up a carriage containing the Earl of Eglinton, who they relieved of a range of valuables, some clothes and a blunderbuss. A pawnbroker was contacted who recognised some of the items as being listed in a broadsheet describing the robberies and informed the authorities. Plunkett disappeared, but Maclaine was arrested. He confessed when charged but on appearing in court put the blame for his transgressions entirely on to the absent Plunkett's shoulders and denied ever being involved in robbery. Nine character witnesses spoke on his behalf but for all that he was extremely unconvincing and was quickly found guilty. Even the well-intentioned statement by Lady Petersham that she regularly received him in her house yet had never known him to take anything that was not his was greeted with a flurry of knowing nudges in court, rather than providing a useful declaration in support of his character. Huge numbers flocked to visit him in the condemned cell but the massive crowds who turned out to watch his execution in 1750 were greatly disappointed. He was so scared that he totally failed to provide any entertainment.

Isaac Darkin was another highwayman very much in the 'gentleman-dandy-paramour' category. He was born in 1740, the son of a prosperous businessman and had a good education. Darkin was a successful scholar until his father died, when the family income plummeted and he was forced to find employment. This very sudden change in his circumstances had a traumatic effect upon the youth who was used to mixing with the sons of very wealthy parents and liked their gracious lifestyle. Darkin did not wish to pursue a life of ill-paid drudgery and therefore decided that becoming a highwayman offered a quick and easy route to riches. Darkin went on to make a name for himself during a short but extremely eventful career.

Darkin first stood trial for his life in 1758 and was sentenced to execution, which was later commuted to fourteen years transportation. He was herded together with dozens of other felons awaiting a ship and found out they were plotting a mass escape during which they would kill their hated jailer. Darkin always seems to have abjured violence but he was an opportunist and he therefore bravely but perfidiously informed on his fellow prisoners. He was given a free pardon on condition that he enlisted as a soldier in an infantry regiment based in Antigua. This was scarcely better than transportation! His career as a soldier was not a success, and lasted only seven weeks. During this time he was disciplined at least three times but it ended when he managed to bribe the captain of a merchant ship to take him back to England.

Darkin took to the road again and ranged widely across southern and central England combining robbery with philandering. He always dressed impeccably, was polite, witty, thoroughly good company and strikingly handsome so it is quite possible that he broke more hearts than he ever lifted purses. He got into innumerable scrapes and appeared in court many times on capital charges but walked free owing to discrepancies in the evidence or on other technicalities. Predictably, in 1761 Darkin's luck ran out, by which time he was firmly cast in the role of popular hero. As he lay in the condemned cell he was visited by large numbers of tearful women pledging to him their undying affection. A vast crowd turned out to witness his execution, for which he dressed immaculately and faced with great courage but no bombast. Darkin was ten days short of his twenty-first birthday.

William Page was a country boy sent to London by his father to learn the haberdashery trade. Like so many before him, he was in turn spellbound and then seduced by the vitality of the capital, its cosmopolitanism and its sharp contrasts between the rich few and the teeming impoverished masses. London gave him a taste for the good life and also made him aware of the many prospects for criminal activity that it harboured. He was a vain young man, determined to cut a dash in all the latest fashions, but when he found that his wages were insufficient to allow him to do this he started to take money from his employer's till. Page was caught out and dismissed, which resulted in his father disowning him and him gaining employment as a liveried servant, a role that he felt was far beneath his dignity.

While on a journey with his employer Page experienced a highway robbery at first hand. It is not known who the highwayman was but he made the act seem so simple and acquired in a couple of minutes what it would have taken Page as a servant two or three years to earn. Page was profoundly impressed, and it did not take him long to make up his mind – he would also become a highwayman. He managed to beg the money for some pistols and the hire of a horse, set off to rob and was rewarded with a total of £4, which happened to be exactly what it had cost him to accumulate the equipment he needed for the venture in the first place. He quickly achieved greater success, took fashionable lodgings and dressed himself in the latest modish finery, joining a select gambling circle and entering polite society.

Page decided to operate rather differently from most highwaymen. First, he taught himself cartography and drew up his own highly detailed maps of London and its surrounding districts. Secondly, he went to work in a phaeton hauled by two horses. At a suitable secluded spot, he would park the phaeton, detach one of the horses, put on his mask and other working togs and then ride to the place he had chosen for the robbery. One day, when he returned from robbing some travellers near Putney, he found to his consternation that the phaeton had disappeared along with his other horse. He rode on and soon found that they had been purloined by a party of haymakers who were engaged in a heated discussion with the very same group of travellers he had just robbed. These indignant travellers were loudly accusing the haymakers of being accomplices of the highwayman. Page reacted quickly to this rather complicated scenario. He threw his highwayman's clothes away and then, clad only in his underwear, he walked up to the group of arguing people declaring that the phaeton was his and accusing the haymakers of having robbed him and taken his outer clothes as well. Everyone involved was brought up before a magistrate who was convinced that the haymakers had indeed stolen the phaeton. Page decided not to press for the prosecution of the haymakers and chastened by the whole affair he sold his phaeton.

Page later held up the notorious rake Lord Ferrers who was called upon to act as chief witness for the prosecution when Page was brought to court charged with highway robbery. Page had astutely researched the many and various shady events of his lordship's past. He unearthed the priceless fact that Ferrers had earlier been excommunicated by a consistory court. In defending himself in court, Page argued that any evidence Ferrers gave would therefore be inadmissible. Choking down his rage, the judge had no option but to let him go free. Page then went into partnership with an old schoolfriend by the name of Darwell and enjoyed several years of such successful robbery that he was able to dress like an aristocrat and drink like a lord. His career ended abruptly in 1758 when a patrol found Page and Darwell in the act of robbery. Darwell was caught and showed the extent of his friendship by turning King's evidence. Page escaped briefly but was soon arrested, tried, sentenced and executed.

In 1766 a macabre event was enacted at Nottingham concerning James Bromage and William Wainer, two highwaymen who had been sentenced to death. They were brought from the Shire Hall to St Mary's Church in High Pavement to hear the execution sermon and after that were required to go into the churchyard to view their graves and to lie in them for a moment to ensure that they would fit. They were then marched off to be executed and a few hours later their bodies were buried in the graves they had only just tried out for size.

There were a number of highwaymen who worked together, but few brothers who joined forces. George and Joseph Weston were an interesting exception to this. Again they were young men from the provinces who moved to London and then erred in their ways to pay for the raffish delights offered by the capital. George swindled his employer and then with his brother frittered the money away on fast living. The fraud was discovered and the Weston brothers had to leave London immediately, and after various adventures arrived in Manchester. George, who was certainly versatile, became a teacher. Not only did he teach but he apparently became a staunch pillar of the community and was appointed High Constable. This post involved too many temptations and he was dismissed for blackmailing innkeepers. The brothers left Manchester and tried their hand at horse-stealing, confidence trickery, forgery and smuggling before deciding to become highwaymen.

Not bothering to work their way up the ladder by risking their necks for a few guineas or the occasional gold watch, the Weston brothers decided to hold up a coach containing the Royal Mail. These coaches were well guarded but the potential rewards for the bold robber were high. The date was January 1781 and without being recognised they escaped with thirty-five mailbags full of bills and banknotes with an estimated value of £15,000, an enormous sum by the standards of the time. The problem for the Westons, of which they were quite aware, was that descriptions of these bills would soon be circulated and therefore they had to be cashed very quickly. George, who was definitely the thinker of the duo, hit on the ingenious ploy of dressing himself as a naval officer with Joseph accompanying him in servant's livery. They then set off at high speed in a hired post-chaise on a roundabout tour of the country, negotiating the bills and banknotes in small numbers in the towns through which they passed. They were first identified after changing a bill in Nottingham and the Post Office authorities hired a team of Bow Street Runners to apprehend them. The Weston brothers led the Runners on a tortuous trail up and down England, always seemingly one jump ahead. They passed through London where their identity was revealed but the Runners were baffled because the trail seemed to go cold.

The brothers had set themselves up in the Sussex seaside town of Winchelsea as men of some financial substance and they were soon moving in fashionable local society. Again George was the more prominent of the two and exuded such an aura of respectability that he was elected a churchwarden, an honour for which he stands out uniquely among highwaymen. However, his tastes remained expensive and although still living undetected under the pseudonym 'William Johnson', he accumulated massive debts that meant that one of his creditors eventually called on the authorities to assist. Two Sheriff's Officers were sent to arrest him and the brothers met them by chance while they were riding outside the town. They were extremely alarmed by this unexpected intrusion into their blissful semi-retirement and so George knocked one of them down with his riding whip and threatened them both with his pistols. The Westons then fled to their sumptuous town house, convinced that the net was closing in. Scooping up a few valuables and necessities, they rode off hotfoot in the direction of London, the place they thought offered the best hiding place. The authorities were now well aware that they were dealing with the notorious Weston brothers. They were traced to London and the persistent Runners eventually caught them in the Soho district.

The Weston brothers appeared in court charged with the robbery of the Royal Mail but the main prosecution witness died at this crucial moment and the case had to be adjourned. George and Joseph remained in Newgate and were visited by their ladyfriends, who brought them a few comforts such as food and drink and, even better, a file and a brace of pistols. They got out of their fetters, overpowered a warder and ran for it, but both were captured within the hour and soon found themselves in a reconvened court. This could not find them guilty of the Royal Mail robbery for lack of evidence but found George guilty of forging endorsements on the stolen bills, which was a capital offence. A similar sentence was passed on Joseph for firing at and injuring a market porter who had tried to stop him when he was escaping from Newgate. The brothers were hanged together at Tyburn on 3 September 1782. Like Dick Turpin who was immortalised by Harrison Ainsworth in his novel *Rookwood*, the Weston brothers also became characters in fiction, appearing in Thackeray's novel *Denis Duval*. While *Rookwood* makes a hero out of Turpin, Thackeray extends no adulation to the Weston brothers. They are portrayed as a pair of singularly graceless villains whose misdeeds only failed to conclude on the scaffold because Thackeray did not complete this particular novel.

One rather unusual highwayman was James or Robert Snooks who ambushed a postboy in Hertfordshire in 1801. He was rewarded with the sum of £1,500 which meant that the authorities soon put the uncommonly high price of £200 on his head, in addition to what by then was the usual payment of £100 under the law. Snooks decided to lie low back in his home town of Hungerford in Berkshire but like so many of his kind, he could not resist bragging and was betrayed by an old school companion. He was hanged at the scene of his crime, Boxmoor Common, in 1802. He went to his death with courage but treated the crowd to a homily on the absolute necessity of strictly observing the Sabbath and always taking heed, as a child, of parental advice. He warned his listeners that failure to do so was the cause of much crime in later life. This was not the kind of speech the spectators had turned out in large numbers to hear and they showed their disapproval by stamping and hissing.

By the late eighteenth century, highwaymen were in decline due to a number of inter-related factors, some of which have already been mentioned. They included the use of rewards as incentives for thief-takers and for ordinary citizens to turn informer. Improved road surfaces, especially on the turnpikes, increased the speed at which travellers and their horses and conveyances could travel. This made them more difficult to stop and also assisted mounted pursuers. Turnpikes were hedged and fenced which greatly restricted the highwayman's freedom of movement. The process of enclosure, an integral part of the drive to increase the output and productivity of agricultural land, also involved laying hedges and fences. These further impeded the ability of a highwayman to evade his pursuers. At the same time the licensing magistrates became more zealous in their efforts to close down inns known to harbour highwaymen and other robbers on the road. The spread of the banking system across the whole country meant that there was much less need for travellers on business and others to carry large amounts of coinage and bank notes, cheques and bills-of-exchange were obviously more difficult for robbers to negotiate. In 1805 the Bow Street Runners set up horse patrols and these could be found along the main roads into London which had long been notorious as the happy hunting grounds of the 'gentlemen of the road'.

It is not surprising that highwaymen continued to thrive for somewhat longer in the provinces. In 1807 the roads of West Sussex around Arundel and Chichester saw considerable activity by a highwayman named Allen, whose victims were mostly farmers returning with wallets bulging after a good day at market. He was eventually shot dead. Not far away the only known father and son highwayman partnership operated, although John Beatson was only the father by legal adoption of his partner-in-crime William Whalley.

It has been emphasised throughout that highway robbery was a young man's game but Beatson made history by riding out as a highwayman for the first time at the ripe old age of seventy. In July 1801 the pair held up the Royal Mail coach at East Grinstead in Sussex and carried off a substantial quantity of bank notes which they needed to negotiate speedily before the details of these notes were circulated around the country. They successfully cashed many of these in the London area, converting them to gold and then bought a horse and gig with a view of going to Ireland. They got as far as Knutsford in Cheshire where they stupidly drew unwelcome attention to themselves by mistreating their horse. As ill luck would have it, this happened just before the coach from London arrived in the town with all the latest news including details of the East Grinstead robbery and of the robbers involved. The description fitted the horse-abusers. A Post Office Surveyor set off after them in the Liverpool direction and they were soon traced and arrested, and found to be in possession of a large number of bank notes. They were taken for trial at Horsham in Sussex and caused a minor sensation by escaping from custody and taking refuge in the town's main sewer from which they apparently were only too glad to be rescued. They were hanged on 7 April 1802.

By the early nineteenth century highwaymen had become an anachronism. However, this did not stop George Cutterman from holding up and robbing travellers in the North Riding of Yorkshire in about 1815. He certainly deserves more than a mere footnote in the history books because after he had been caught and taken to York to stand trial he persuaded his somewhat lax guards to remove his handcuffs. Minutes later he leapt out of the coach and sprinted out of sight and into oblivion. He was never heard of again. As late as 1850 the 'Hanham and Cock Road Gang' carried out numerous violent robberies in the country areas surrounding Bristol. They ignored the gallant highwayman tradition and what they lacked in social finesse they made up for with extreme brutality. They made a point of preventing their victims from calling for help by stuffing their mouths full of dirt or throttling them. These vicious thugs had little in common with such urbane highwaymen as Jack Rann, James Maclaine or Isaac Darkin.

NINE

Road Travel in Georgian Times

By the beginning of the eighteenth century Britain had a road system but its inadequacies added enormously to the cost of transport and to the price of goods. These problems were retarding the country's industrial development at a time when the growth of commerce and the needs of public administration increased the demand for and amount of travel. The most effective way of travelling was on horseback and in favourable conditions distances of 30 to 70 miles could be covered in a day. Horse-drawn wagons carrying goods and passengers lumbered along at speeds rarely exceeding 3 miles an hour and pack trains of mules carrying all kinds of articles moved even more slowly. The poor condition of the roads is exemplified by Daniel Defoe's description of an old woman being drawn to church near Lewes in Sussex by six oxen because horses would not have been able to move through the mire. Even around the capital the situation was no better. In 1736 an anonymous writer complained of the state of the road between Kensington and London, 'It is grown so infamously bad that we live here in the same solitude as we should do if cast on a rock in the middle of the ocean, and all the Londoners tell us that there is between them and us a great impassable gulf of mud.'

In 1706 Parliament sanctioned a new system which allowed a group of trustees to borrow money to finance road improvements along a specified section of road and to levy charges from road-users. These 'Turnpike Trustees' fenced off the designated piece of road and erected toll-levying facilities at both ends and where any other roads joined along the way. The income from tolls was to be used to improve and maintain that particular section of highway. The turnpike idea took root and by the 1830s, the beginning of the railway age, England and Wales had about 1,100 turnpike trusts which between them administered 22,000 miles of main road. This was something like 20 per cent of the rural road mileage. The great drawback of the turnpikes was that the trusts were purely local bodies and no attempt was made to develop a national system of turnpiked highways. It meant that a long journey was likely to involve both turnpiked and ordinary road, the contrast between the two being very obvious. However, the turnpike system did enable road surfaces to be significantly improved and on a few major roads, such as those from London to Edinburgh, Manchester, Shrewsbury, Bristol and Portsmouth, virtually the whole route was turnpiked.

Daniel Defoe, writing in 1724, was impressed with the improvement of the Essex roads as a result of the building of turnpikes: 'The great road from London . . . towards Ipswich and Harwich, is the most worn with wagons, carts and carriages; and with infinite droves of black cattle, hogs and sheep of any road in England . . . These roads were formerly deeply rutted, in times of flood dangerous, and at other times in winter scarce passable, they are now so firm, so safe, so easy to travellers, and carriages as well as cattle . . . This was first done by the help of a turnpike, set up by Act of Parliament, about the year 1697 . . .'

Turnpikes were not always seen in a positive light at the time. New ones were extremely unpopular with local road users who understandably resented having to pay tolls to travel on roads along which they had previously enjoyed free passage. This antipathy to turnpikes went so far as to spark off the destruction of gates and physical assaults on turnpike employees. For example, at Bristol in 1727, 1731 and 1748 gangs of farmers and miners destroyed the gates and set fire to toll houses, in one case brutally murdering a tollkeeper. Hostility to turnpikes culminated in the 'Rebecca Riots' of 1842–3 in South Wales. These were orchestrated by a secret society and were a protest against the burden of tolls at a time of great economic hardship, as well as a demonstration against the hated Poor Law Amendment Act of 1834. The rioters disguised themselves in women's clothes and called themselves 'Rebecca's Daughters' after the prophecy in Genesis 24:60 that Rebecca's seed should possess the 'gate of those which hate them'. The inauguration of the turnpikes helped to reduce the dangers of highway robbery as one of the gatekeeper's duties was to inform the authorities and the travelling public if highwaymen were known to be in the area. Additionally, the fencing and gating of the turnpikes made it highly impractical for highway robbers to use these roads because if they did so they almost became trapped.

Competition meant that coaching companies were always trying to accelerate their services. This may have deterred highwaymen but higher speeds were very much a mixed blessing because they increased the likelihood of accidents. There were collisions, horses sometimes bolted or harness broke and faster travel heightened the dangers attendant on coachmen falling asleep, a not uncommon occurrence when they had slaked their thirsts at a succession of inns and posting houses along the route. Sometimes passengers even toppled off the top of coaches and descending hills was a particular problem. Until brakes came into use in the 1830s, the guard had the unenviable task of leaping down from the coach and slipping a skid under the nearside front wheel as the coach approached a steep downhill incline. On one occasion a coach approaching Hounslow at excessive speed slid off the road into a pond, with one passenger being drowned. In fog, a coach passing through a seaside town went out of control and plunged off the quay, resulting in ten passengers being drowned. A coach from Cheltenham to Hereford was proceeding at breakneck speed in exceptionally heavy rain when the coachman failed to spot that a bridge had been washed away. The coach, horses and passengers all plunged into the cataract. In 1784 the Hertford coach overturned, the cause being the weight of twenty-five people riding on the top of the vehicle combined with excessive speed. Given the number of coaches tearing up and down Britain's roads when competition was at its height, it is surprising that that there were so few disasters on the road.

In the eighteenth century the long-distance stagecoach system developed rapidly, reaching its peak in the 1830s, when it then succumbed quickly to railway competition. An extremely comprehensive network of services was built up and the comfort and speed of coaches were taken to the limits practical for this form of transport. The stagecoaches themselves and the large industry that arose to service the horses and conveyances and to provide hospitality for the travellers engendered a sense of affection and well-being in many observers:

As we drove into the great gateway of the inn, I saw on one side the light of the rousing kitchen fire beckoning through a window. I entered and admired the neatness and honest enjoyment that is the kitchen of an English inn . . . hams, tongues and great flitches of bacon were suspended from the ceiling; a smoke-jack made its ceaseless clanking beside the fireplace; and a clock ticked in one corner. A well-scoured deal table extended along one side of the kitchen, with a cold round of beef and other viands upon it, surrounded by foaming tankards . . . trim housemaids were hurrying backwards and forwards under the direction of a fresh-faced bustling landlady who still seized an occasional moment to exchange a flippant word and have a rallying laugh with the group around the fire.

Similar sentiments are expressed in George Eliot's novel *Felix Holt, the Radical* (1866): 'Five and thirty years ago the glory had not yet departed from the old coach roads; the great roadside inns were still brilliant with well-polished tankards, the smiling glances of pretty barmaids and the repartee of jocose ostlers; the mail still announced

A young woman pleading at the trial of James Maclaine in 1750. Maclaine stands in the dock.

The London to Devonport Royal Mail coach 'Quicksilver' outside the Star and Garter inn, *c.* 1870.

A contemporary woodcut depicting Dick Turpin at full gallop evading his pursuers.

Dick Turpin holds up fellow highwayman Tom King. This melodramatic depiction obscures the fact that Turpin and King quickly established a rapport from which a very successful working partnership developed.

Dick Turpin rides past corpses hanging on a gibbet during his legendary ride from London to York, from Lloyd's edition of *Claude Duval*, plate 6.

Harrison Ainsworth (1805–82), the Victorian novelist who wrote an account of Turpin's adventures in *Rookwood*, published 1824.

itself by the merry notes of the horn; the hedge-cutter or the rick-thatcher still knew the exact hour by the unfailing yet meteoric apparition of the pea-green Tally-Ho or the yellow Independent . . .' Tobias Smollett in his little-known novel *Sir Launcelot Greaves* (1762) warms to the same theme when describing the inn-kitchen: 'It was paved with red bricks, remarkably clean, furnished with three or four windsor chairs, adorned with shining plates of pewter, and copper saucepans nicely scoured that even dazzled the eyes of the beholder, while a cheerful fire of sea coal blazed in the chimney.'

William Cobbett was not an easy man to please. In his *Rural Rides* published in 1830 he fulminated against the economic and social changes he considered to be undermining the quality of English life. However he had a soft spot for the coaching industry: 'Next to a fox-hunt the finest sight in England is a stage coach just ready to start . . . in a stage coach you see what man is capable of performing. The vehicle itself; the harness all so complete and so neatly arranged, so strong and clean and good; the beautiful horses, impatient to be off; the inside full, and the outside covered, in every part, with men, women and children, boxes, bags, bundles; the coachman, taking his reins in one hand and the whip in the other, gives the signal with his foot, and away they go, at the rate of seven miles an hour.' The writer Thomas de Quincey (1785–1859) best known for his *Confessions of an Opium-Eater*, clearly loved the experience of coach travel: 'Seated on the old mail-coach, we needed no evidence out of ourselves to indicate the velocity. The vital experience of the glad animal sensibilities made doubts impossible. We heard our speed, we saw it, we felt it as a thrilling; and this speed was not the product of blind insensate agencies that had no sympathy to give, but was incarnated in the fiery eyeballs of the noblest among brutes, in his dilated nostril, spasmodic muscles, and thunder-beating hooves.'

These quotations all convey a strong sense of the affection and regard for the coaches and the inns they stopped at. The height of the ambition of countless young men, and many not so young, was to ride with the coachman and perhaps take over the reins for a short distance. Coachmen were heroes whose swagger and hauteur every schoolboy tried to emulate and whose job they envied in much the same way that later generations of boys and men admired engine drivers. There is little doubt that the coaching system at its peak stirred the imagination in a way that was perhaps not seen again until the London, Midland and Scottish and the London and North Eastern Railways launched their competing streamlined steam-hauled express trains from London to Scotland in the 1930s.

The American man of letters Washington Irving (1783–1859) gave this description of a coachman in 1819: 'A broad, full face, curiously mottled red; he is swelled into jolly dimensions by frequent potations of malt liquours and his bulk is still further increased by a multiplicity of coats in which he is buried like a cauliflower, the upper one reaching to his heels. He wears a broad-brimmed low-crowned hat; a huge roll of coloured handkerchief about his neck; knowingly knotted and tucked in at the bosom; and has in summer time a large bouquet of flowers in his buttonhole; the present, most probably, of some enamoured country lass.' Not everyone, however, was so favourably impressed by the coaching industry. One writer grumbled, '. . . the usual coach dinner – a coarse fat leg of mutton, roasted to a cinder, a huge joint of boiled beef, underdone, and gritty cabbage'. This view is echoed by another traveller: 'The innkeepers are insolent, the ostlers are sulky, the chambermaids are impertinent; the meat is tough, the wine is foul, the linen is dirty, and the knives are never cleaned . . . I look upon an inn as the seat of all roguery, profaneness and debauchery . . . for the sake of hasty gain, innkeepers hire horrid servants and provide but bad provisions and poisonous liquors.' Viscount Torrington writing in the 1780s gives a very similar view: 'My sheets were damp and the blankets so dirty and stinking and the room smelt so strongly of putresence that I slept very little, though I took off the sheets and employed all the brandy, nearly a pint, in purifying the room and sprinkling the quilt and the blankets . . .'

Many coach travellers complained about the company that they were forced to endure within the very close confines of the stagecoach itself. The hazards included the portly gentleman who paid for just one seat while in reality occupying two, the querulous, peevish traveller venting his spleen on everybody and everything, the garrulous know-all providing a running commentary on every wearisome subject under the sun, the drunkard, the snorer and the amorously inclined lecher. One unknown traveller made a very pithy comment: 'My fellow-passenger had the highest of all terrestrial qualities which for me a fellow-passenger can possess – he was silent.' An additional hazard was the guard who wished to entertain the passengers by blowing the coach-horn incessantly, others who performed continuously on the bugle and those who believed they were virtuoso singers. A traveller recalls the everyday hazards of coach travel: 'I did climb to the outside seat I had taken, and the guard blew his horn and we drove off. The day was fine . . . But when we had covered scarce half our journey . . . the off leader shied at a hen flying across the road, and before we had scarce time to think what was afoot, the Coach lurches, and then tumbles into a ditch, the road being soft with mud at that point. The ditch was deep but none was hurt bad; but two women inside began to scream most piercing, being badly shook in their wits . . .'

It made good sense to book a seat beforehand. A gentleman from Edinburgh of very ample girth made a habit of booking two seats every time he travelled so as to ensure his own comfort. He must have been greatly disconcerted on the occasion that he arrived at the coaching inn to find that his servant had indeed reserved two seats for him but one seat was inside and the other on the top of the coach! A German traveller did not enjoy the experience of riding on the coach roof: 'The getting up alone was at the risk of one's life, and when I was up, I was obliged to sit just at the corner of the coach with nothing to hold on to but a sort of little handle fastened on the side and the moment we set off, I fancied I saw certain death await me! At last the being continuously in fear of my life became insupportable . . . I crept from the top of the coach and got snug into the basket. As long as we went up hill it was easy and pleasant. I was almost asleep among the trunks and packages; but how was the case altered when we came to go down hill, then all the trunks and parcels began, as it were, to dance around me, and I every moment received such violent blows that I thought my last hour was come!'

Travellers on horseback, by postchaise or private carriage could avoid many of the perils that beset travellers by public coach – instead they 'posted'. Many wayside inns kept horses that could be hired to draw a private carriage onwards to another posting house. Highwaymen, however, were particularly interested in this expensive form of travel because those who used it were likely to be well-to-do. The threat of theft and robbery was ever-present, and it was not just highwaymen who exacted plunder from travellers. Much of the theft that took place was less obvious. Gangs of pickpockets frequented the yards of coaching inns and found rich pickings in the disorganised mêlée that occurred, particularly at busy times.

Sometimes pickpockets even bought tickets to ride in coaches and found easy pickings especially on hot days when passengers replete with food and drink dozed off in the stuffy interior of the coach. When the coach stopped at a wayside inn, travellers often alighted, stretched their legs or went in for food and drink. They were often careless with their parcels and other possessions and no sooner had they turned their back than these were spirited away by opportunist thieves. In 1820 the Bristol mail coach was robbed of parcels with contents worth about £400. Four men booked the inside of the coach to themselves from Bath and had silently broken through the fabric of the carriage, seized the strongbox under the driver's seat, unlocked it, removed the contents and then replaced it. Other highly skilled robbers used a skeleton key to open a double lock and a padlock under the driver's seat of the Gravesend coach in 1825. Robbery of a different kind was carried out by coachmen, waiters and all the others who ministered to travellers' needs. They expected tips and the way in which they solicited for these often amounted to demanding money with menaces.

The peak of the coaching system was short-lived and was reached in about 1835 when there were no fewer than 700 mail coaches in operation and some 3,300 stagecoaches. In the late 1830s 1,476 long-haul coaches left London daily, with 50 coaches running daily between London and Brighton and 22 to Birmingham. So great was the business at the height of the coaching era that at Hounslow, the first and last changing place for coaches and carriages travelling into and out of London on the road to Bath and Bristol, the coaching inns between them kept a total of no less than 2,500 horses. In the 1820s, the upkeep of these horses was estimated at £2 per week, which meant that in terms of horses alone £5,000 circulated in the town weekly. The coaching industry was a major employer, the care of horses being particularly labour intensive and there were many jobs in industries dependent on coaching such as coach-building, harness-making, smithying and wheel-wrights. Just as the early nineteenth century was the peak of the coaching industry, it also marks the start of the decline of the highwayman's predatory activities.

TEN

Dick Turpin

Of all the highway robbers, it is probably Dick Turpin who has the greatest number of legends, myths and misunderstandings attached to his name. These developed even when he was alive because he seemed the very embodiment of the dashing highwayman and later when he became a hero in literary fiction. There are what seem to be unimpeachable facts such as the place and date of his birth and his death, but a caveat should be issued for most of the other details of his life that are outlined below.

Turpin was born at Hempstead in Essex, not far from Saffron Walden, in 1705 and the parish register confirms his baptism. The village is of more than national interest because the parish church contains a number of monuments to the Harvey family, including William Harvey, 1578–1657, who discovered the circulation of the blood. Turpin's father was landlord of what is now The Rose and Crown in the village, among the oldest continuously licensed pubs in Britain. He was also a butcher and he insisted on his son gaining at least a rudimentary education. Dick was taught to read and write and this was to prove significant at a later and extremely crucial time in his life. Turpin completed an apprenticeship in the butchery trade, at either Whitechapel, Waltham Abbey in Hertfordshire or Thaxted in Essex. He was then twenty-one and was soon to marry a young lady whose name in some accounts is given as Rose Palmer and in others as Elizabeth Millington. She was the daughter of a publican who ran The Rose and Crown at

Enfield. This conflicting information is typical of the confusion surrounding Turpin's life.

Turpin made a promising start in the butchery trade and gained an enviable reputation for the quality of his meat. His problem was that he insisted on enjoying the good things of life although he was unable to afford them. Consequently, he quickly got into serious debt. Soon after he had opened up his business there was an outbreak of sheep rustling in the neighbourhood and a local farmer traced two of his missing beasts through Turpin's abattoir to a tannery at Waltham Abbey. This is hardly surprising because Turpin had found that producing veal cutlets, dressing chump chops and being polite to customers who clearly despised tradesmen like him was no kind of occupation for a young man who craved excitement and an easy route to wealth. It had occurred to him that the best way of cutting the costs of his business would be to cut out the middleman and rustle or steal the raw material for his butchery business. Rather than staying to face the consequences, however, Turpin left the district knowing that what had happened had ended his career in the butchery trade.

Turpin headed for the Essex coast, and was supported by his wife until he began to make some money through his involvement in a smuggling gang. It seems that whatever he earned was never enough to keep him in the lifestyle to which he aspired and so, totally lacking scruples, he graduated to robbing his supposed colleagues by masquerading as a Revenue Officer. His efforts in this direction were unappreciated by both the Revenue Service and the smuggling fraternity and in due course he wisely decided to decamp. He was probably lucky to leave the area alive and headed for Waltham Forest, now known as Epping Forest. At that time this area was a heavily wooded, ill-frequented and remote district which was close enough to London to offer rich criminal pickings and act as a refuge for a variety of miscreants whose activities had placed them outside the law.

Here Turpin joined a gang of deer-rustlers generally known as 'Gregory's Gang' after their leader. Turpin's expertise in butchery proved invaluable to the gang because it made sense to cut up the carcasses before taking them to London where there were shady game dealers prepared to buy but ask no questions. Eventually, the gang branched out and started breaking into churches, stealing chalices, patens and other pieces of church plate, and housebreaking. They also brutally assaulted and even raped the occupants and wantonly destroyed their property. When the victims were slow to reveal the location of their valuables, the gang jogged their memories with casual torture. A well-known picture shows a robber placing an old woman on a fire and uttering the immortal words, 'God damn your blood, you old bitch, if you won't tell us I'll set your arse on the grate.' The robber is supposed to have been Turpin but there is no evidence that he was any more brutal than other gang members. It is also claimed that they poured boiling water over an old man to force him to reveal where he kept his money.

'Gregory's Gang' acquired a well-deserved reputation for exceptional nastiness and a large reward was offered for information leading to their apprehension. This announcement was spiced with the tempting offer of a free pardon for any gang member prepared to turn King's evidence. Carousing one evening in a Westminster tavern, some gang members were suddenly set upon by the authorities and Gregory and the others were caught. It is said that Turpin evaded capture by jumping out of an upstairs window and that he landed astride his waiting horse before galloping off pell-mell to safety. Turpin lived to see most of his companions hanged at Tyburn after one of the gang turned King's evidence. He managed to evade the authorities but had a high price on his head.

This experience provided Turpin with a salutary lesson and he resolved to stop working as part of a large gang. He teamed up with another survivor of 'Gregory's Gang', known as 'Rowden the Pewterer' and they took to the road as highwaymen. In 1735 they carried out several bold daylight robberies around Wandsworth, Barnes and Putney and in the Blackheath area. The robberies ascribed to Turpin and Rowden certainly carried the stamp of professionalism. They employed no unnecessary violence and they forced their victims to dismount, removing the bridles from their horses and turning the animals loose so that their victims had some distance to walk before they could raise the alarm. They seem to have worked well together but it appears that Rowden left for pastures new, although it is not known why, and then reports started coming in of 'Turpin the Butcher', as he became known, holding up travellers single-handed in the Twickenham area. It is worth mentioning that few highwaymen wore the little fancy dress black masks over their eyes with which they are often portrayed in popular fiction. They usually sported large pieces of dark cloth covering the lower parts of their faces and tied at the back of their necks. With their large-brimmed riding hats on, little of their faces could be seen. Their eyes, their voices, their general appearance and their mannerisms might give them away, however.

An event soon occurred that was the very stuff of legend. One evening Turpin was lurking around the Cambridge road out of London when he sighted a solitary traveller approaching on a fine horse and he promptly ordered him to stand and deliver. To his amazement the stranger was not in the least taken aback and actually called on him to do precisely the same. It is said that the stranger laughed uproariously on being challenged and declared: 'What, dog eat dog? Come, come, Brother Turpin, if you don't know me, I know you well, and shall be glad of your company.' This is how Turpin is said to have made the acquaintance of Tom King, himself a highwayman of some notoriety. The meeting led to one of the best-known partnerships among highwaymen. Instead of engaging in a shoot-out, each man obviously liked the cut of the other's jib and they got on well from the start. Turpin proved a willing pupil for the lessons that the more experienced King could teach him about the techniques of the highwayman. They decided to make a hideaway in a cave in the depths of Epping Forest to the north-east of London which would, however, be close to a number of highways that offered the potential for rich pickings. Turpin's wife brought food and other necessities to their secret lair. Soon Turpin and King were annoying the authorities around London with a series of audacious and lucrative robberies.

It was inevitable that Turpin's and King's hideaway would not remain secret for long. On several occasions posses chased them into the forest but did not manage to locate their hiding place. The Forest was much larger then than now and the cave was cunningly hidden, but they were well aware that the cave might be discovered. They lured posses away from the area on wild-goose chases and even, when the ground was soft and hoofprints could have given them away, rode their horses randomly long distances through the mud creating a spoor that was incomprehensible to any trackers. However, the price on the heads of both Turpin and King tempted a keeper in Epping Forest and an accomplice to try to capture them. Turpin was alone when the bounty hunters crept up on the cave, but he responded quickly, however, and shot and killed one of them. The price on Turpin's head went up again – he was now worth £200. He decided to evacuate the cave, although not before he had spent an uncomfortable time high up in a tree while a pack of bloodhounds roamed the forest floor trying vainly to sniff him out. The newspapers made great play of this episode and of Turpin's audacious and continuing villainy.

The partnership of Turpin and King was highly successful and it is said that they only ever had one row. This occurred at Bungay in Suffolk when they came across two young women who had just sold a load of corn for £14. For Turpin the idea of stealing this money appealed strongly because it was so simple. However, King was known for his gallantry and he insisted that these young women be allowed to proceed unmolested. Nevertheless, Turpin lagged behind and proceeded to rob the hapless girls. King found out and this episode caused a rift between the two men that took some time to heal. Eventually the friendship was restored and Turpin and King went on to many other adventures, some of which illustrate the hazards of the highwayman's life. Near Epping one afternoon they apprehended a private coach. The gentleman to whom the coach belonged was very aware of the dangers of highwaymen in this district and had taken the wise precaution of equipping himself with a range of firearms, all loaded, cocked and ready to fire. As Turpin came alongside the coach, he peered in while the man poked the barrel out of the window and fired at point-blank range. Luckily for Turpin the powder merely flashed in the pan. An enraged Turpin then fired blindly into the dim inner recesses of the coach. Fate that day was impartial – at least his weapon actually fired but the ball passed right though the vehicle between the plucky owner and his wife. This episode clearly disconcerted King and Turpin who then rode off empty handed.

The Turpin and King partnership came to an abrupt and unexpected end in May 1737. Turpin, King and an associate named Potter were riding into London and as they were nearing The Green Man at Epping found that Turpin's horse was showing signs of discomfort. A rider came towards them, a Mr Major, astride a splendid horse called 'Whitestockings'. Turpin told him to dismount and hand the beast over, which was foolhardy because 'Whitestockings' was a very well-known steeplechaser of distinctive appearance. He compounded the misjudgment by also appropriating Major's riding whip, which bore his name. A crestfallen Major then went to The Green Man and told the landlord, a Mr Boyes or Bayes, what had happened. Boyes saw the stamp of Turpin on this escapade and advised Major to have some handbills printed and circulated offering a handsome reward for the recovery of the horse. A few days later, Boyes heard that 'Whitestockings' had been seen in stables attached to The Red Lion in Whitechapel. Boyes, who had some scores of his own to settle with Turpin, galloped off hotfoot to Whitechapel where he recognised the horse. He summoned a constable and they hid away to watch who came to reclaim 'Whitestockings'. A man turned up and they seized him but it was not one of the trio they were looking for. It was Matthew King,

Tom's brother who, despite the fact that he was brandishing Major's whip, said he knew nothing about the horse having been stolen and had merely been told to fetch it. Matthew, who was visibly quaking in his boots, could not cope with this totally unexpected turn of events and was easily persuaded to lead Boyes and the constable to where they could find Turpin and the others.

What happened next is extremely unclear, there being so many varying accounts. Apparently, Boyes spotted King who in turn recognised the landlord and fired at him. Boyes then rode up to King who called on Turpin to shoot him. Turpin loosed off a shot but somehow he managed to miss Boyes and hit his friend Tom King instead, injuring him mortally. Some accounts say that it was Matthew King who was hit by Turpin's bullet. Whoever it was that Turpin had shot, it seems that he was full of contrition and soon afterwards he told a friendly publican that all this unpleasantness was the fault of Boyes who had caused him to lose the best companion he ever had. Other accounts say that Tom survived, but there is no record of Tom King being hanged and it seems unlikely that he would have emerged unscathed and simply faded away. It has even been suggested that Boyes killed King in a fight in prison.

Turpin got away and one account says that he was so appalled by what had happened that he retired to the country and took a smallholding. Saddened and chastened as he must have been by the loss of his companion, Turpin nevertheless was quickly on the road again and carrying out a series of audacious robberies that led to an even greater sum being placed on his head. This made life extremely hazardous for Turpin because his appearance was well known and he presented a tempting prize to those who wanted to get rich quickly by alerting the authorities to his whereabouts. He certainly had some close shaves. He took lodgings in London but someone unknown must have informed on him. The authorities broke into the house and the landlady who was loyal to him managed to delay them long enough to enable Turpin, who had been asleep, to throw on a few clothes, climb out of an upstairs window and make his way over the rooftops and down to safety in the street. It was about this time, when highway robbery was probably at its peak, that Turpin gained his reputation as something of a 'Scarlet Pimpernel'. He apparently managed to carry out robberies in two or more places at the same time and yet to outwit the most ingenious efforts made by the authorities to bring him to justice. Turpin must have chuckled when he read newspaper accounts of his arrest and imprisonment awaiting trial. Then, when his depredations were at their height and the mere mention of his name was enough to cause nervous travellers to come out in goose pimples, Turpin suddenly disappeared.

Rumours were rife and as usual those who ventured most knew least. He was reported stealing horses and sheep near Long Sutton in Lincolnshire where someone answering his description narrowly missed arrest. Then the scenario shifts to the East Riding of Yorkshire around Beverley and a certain John Palmer who had moved into the area, from Lincolnshire it was said. He was in business as a horse-dealer, the eighteenth-century equivalent of a second-hand car-dealer, but he always seemed to have plenty of money. He affected the style of a country gentleman, hobnobbing with the local gentry, but there were those who felt that he did not quite fit in socially. These intuitions were startlingly confirmed in October 1738 when Palmer, returning with a party from a shoot, suddenly shot his landlord's gamecock when it strutted across the road in front of his horse. Another version of the story says that he stole the gamecock. Now a gamecock was no mere farmyard fowl but an asset that could bring its owner considerable wealth at a time when cockfighting had never been more popular. Palmer's action seemed entirely pointless and provocative and when another member of the party pointed this out, Palmer boorishly threatened to shoot him too.

A complaint was made to the local magistrate and Palmer was arrested. He was bailed to appear at the next quarter sessions but he could not provide the necessary surety from any of the local gentry so he was placed in the local house of correction pending further investigations. These revealed that Palmer was wanted elsewhere in Yorkshire and also in Lincolnshire for a string of offences involving the rustling of livestock, especially horses, but also that nothing whatever seemed to be known about his life before he arrived in the county. Clearly there were questions about Palmer that needed answering and he was therefore transferred to the gaol at York Castle. The mysteries surrounding Palmer deepened when a witness came forward to say that Palmer had recently shown him a cache of firearms that included many of the types favoured by highwaymen. Some were beginning to say that there might be a connection between Palmer and the notorious Turpin who had so unexpectedly and completely disappeared. He resided in the gaol for a few months during which time he wrote to his brother or his brother-in-law, asking him to act as a character witness at the forthcoming trial, and this letter proved to be his undoing. He omitted to pay the postage and his relation, not recognising the handwriting, refused to pay. Back the letter went to the local post office at Hempstead, Turpin's parish of origin where, by the faintest of chances, it was recognised by the very person who had taught him his letters twenty or more years earlier, a schoolmaster named John Smith. It can only be supposed that the highwayman had very distinctive handwriting and that Smith was both sure of himself and anxious to secure the reward money. A local magistrate was alerted and things moved very quickly.

Here was the country's most notorious highwayman incarcerated in York Prison for the mundane crime of horse stealing. The offence was a capital one, however, and upon being found guilty, Turpin was sentenced to death. Ancient proverbs about it being as well to be hanged for a sheep as for a lamb come to mind at this point but here in real life was Turpin the highwayman about to be executed for the theft of a horse. The authorities could scarcely believe their luck on discovering that the prisoner Palmer was in fact the notorious Turpin. He conducted himself with admirable sang-froid, both in his cell, where he had a large number of visitors who enjoyed wining, dining and joking with him, and during his last moments on the scaffold. A chaplain in the prison wrote of Turpin: 'He seemed to pay but little regard to the serious remonstrances and admonitions of the reverend gentlemen who attended him, and whatever remorse he had on his conscience for his villainies, he kept them to himself.' Determined to impress, Turpin bought an entire new suit of fustian and a pair of expensive new shoes for the occasion and paid five mourners, sporting black hatbands and mourning gloves, to follow his cart to the gallows. He was executed at the Knavesmire, the traditional place where felons were executed just outside York, on 7 April 1739, at the age of thirty-three. He demonstrated his courage by chatting genially with the hangman and the crowd, although close eyewitnesses said that they distinctly saw his right knee tremble. He calmly and quietly took the option of throwing himself off the ladder, expiring within minutes.

Turpin's body was taken first of all to The Blue Boar Inn in Castlegate, York, and the next day it was buried at St George's Church. An attempt was made to disinter the body and sell it to teachers of anatomy and surgery at some distant medical school but the villains were seen and chased and, becoming hard-pressed, they unceremoniously dumped Turpin's uncomplaining corpse in a handy back garden. The cadaver was recovered and restored to its grave but then covered in quicklime. This may sound disrespectful but would have had the very practical effect of rendering it useless to any other 'resurrection-men'.

The rumbustious, swashbuckling Turpin was the hero of numerous legends and ballads. The aura of romance that surrounds him is largely the product of fiction, especially the pen of Harrison Ainsworth, a now largely forgotten but once widely read novelist. His first novel *Rookwood*, published in 1824, gave a very fanciful and imaginative account with highly distinctive illustrations by George Cruikshank of Turpin's activities, including his headlong gallop from London to York on 'Black Bess' in order to establish an alibi. This ride never took place but the myths and fantasies about Turpin had appeared and multiplied well before Ainsworth created his own version of events. Here was the dashing, debonair, devil-may-care highwayman of whom fantasies and legends are made and it helped that he was also possibly the most successful of all the highwaymen, evading attempts to capture him for so many years. He was resourceful and he was brave and legend has it that single-handed he simultaneously stopped and robbed two coaches, which between them contained no less than twenty passengers. With a high price on his head, there were few he could trust but it says something about Turpin that nobody effectively betrayed him while he was at liberty. This may have been because they were scared of the consequences but it could be because he was actually respected, although it is difficult to identify anything about him that is particularly admirable.

In real life Dick Turpin seems to have been a vicious, highly able horse-thief, highway robber and murderer to whom gallantry and concern for his victims was unknown. He was tall by the standards of the time and strongly built and his facial appearance was not helped by the fact he was severely pockmarked. It is unlikely that Turpin bandied witticisms with his victims or that he even had a roguish twinkle in his eye, and he does not seem to have allowed his eye to rove in a predatory way over the female sex in the fashion that we often associate with highwaymen.

Quite what Turpin's appeal was is difficult to define. However, there is scarcely an ancient inn on the roads out of London to the east, west or north that does not have its fables about Turpin, who either ate, drank or slept there or used the place as his headquarters. There are innumerable hostelries that claim that Turpin stopped off there briefly while under close pursuit to have his horse's shoes reshod so that they pointed backwards. Turpin is then supposed to have hurried away on the redoubtable 'Black Bess', giving his pursuers the slip as they set off eagerly following the hoof-marks that had led them there in the first place. Never was there a better example of the willing suspension of disbelief. The wide dispersal and frequent occurrence of this particular story should not be taken as evidence of its authenticity.

Turpin's resting place can be viewed in the churchyard of St George in York but it seems that his spirit still roams free. Many sites along the Great North Road report his tricorn-hatted, caped and spurred figure astride the ever-faithful 'Black Bess', lurking hopefully by the roadside waiting for well-heeled travellers. There are those who swear that he regularly rides a phantom horse down Traps Hill in Essex, not far from Epping Forest. Clinging on to Turpin's form, literally like grim death, is a spectral woman who he is said to have tortured and murdered for her money.

It is probable that Turpin never owned a horse called 'Black Bess' and it is almost definite that he did not make the dash between London and York to create an alibi. This is often ascribed to William Nevison (*see* pp. 81–2) but it could have been carried out by a highwayman named Harris. He was recognised while carrying out a robbery although this time the location was somewhere in Surrey. He likewise rode to York and made his way to a public bowling green where he made a point of asking a number of gentlemen for the time, saying that he wanted to check whether his own timepiece was accurate. In his case the court was unimpressed and things looked bad for Harris until a wealthy and influential aristocrat interceded on his behalf. Harris lived happily ever after, first of all setting up a fencing school and then having the good fortune to marry a wealthy heiress. This story bears too many similarities to those of Nevison and Turpin to make it entirely credible. The inclusion of the sympathetic aristocrat and the heiress stretch the plausibility even further.

Ainsworth makes the most of the ride to York, creating a swashbuckling and, eventually, tear-jerking episode. Turpin rides hell-for-leather out of London and, remarkably, brandishing his pistols in his hands and gripping the bridle at the same time, clears the Hornsey Tollgate in one mighty, inspired bound. Turpin careers up the Great North Road calling in a number of inns en route. Dramatically, he reaches York, 196 miles from London, just as the Minster bells sound the hour of six when, to his total consternation, tragedy strikes. His faithful steed has literally reached her journey's end – 'Black Bess' collapses with exhaustion and expires quickly, but not before Turpin, beside himself with sorrow, looks lovingly into her glazing-over eyes and reverentially kisses her foam-flecked lips. He then delivers a heartfelt, deeply touching valediction for the horse and the benefit of any passers-by who cared to listen. With some difficulty the mourning Turpin is separated from his beloved mount by a gypsy who agrees to dispose of the horse's inert form. Then our hero suddenly remembers why he has put himself and his horse to so much trouble. Turpin rushes off breathlessly to the bowling green where he ensures that he is seen by as many of York's leading citizens as possible.

Any resemblance between this account and historical actuality is of course purely coincidental. Does it matter? Ainsworth claimed that he wrote the whole story of the ride to York, amounting to nearly 20,000 words, in a day and a night. This is not easy to believe but he was a novelist, not a historian and people flocked in tens of thousands to buy, read and reread what at the time was considered to be an exciting adventure story. It would have been churlish to point out how unlikely it is that such a journey could have been performed by just one horse in that length of time.

The legendary Turpin was a handsome highwayman of the gentlemanly kind. Brave, almost buccaneering, he was admired for his exploits in cocking a snook at authority and robbing the rich. Destitute, frail widows and farm labourers down on their luck, so it was averred, had nothing to fear from this 'gentleman of the road'. In fact, when appealed to, he might prove only too happy to fling the odd coin their way. This kind of behaviour almost certainly bore no resemblance to the activities of the real Turpin. However, if a now largely forgotten Victorian novelist chose to take Turpin's story and weave a tale based on a number of existing legends, producing a best-selling novel, then the historian is provided with many interesting insights into the Victorian interpretation of the man who was probably the most famous highway robber in British history.

ELEVEN

Policing Before Robert Peel

The word 'constable' was a Norman term that by the middle of the thirteenth century came to refer to increasingly important public functionaries who had 'hands-on' duties to police the community and who were supervised by the magistrates or justices of the peace. These constables are lampooned by Shakespeare in the characters of 'Dogberry' in *Much Ado About Nothing* and 'Elbow' in *Measure for Measure*. These may be early examples of the common theme in British humour of parodying law-enforcers, or it may represent the popular perception that such officers were bumbling incompetents. The office of constable became increasingly burdensome in the seventeenth century because in addition to the task of maintaining the peace was the enforcement of legislation concerning church attendance, measures against drunkards and vagrants and various other duties. London constables were not known for their zeal. Some paid others to carry out their duties or obtained a reduction in their period of tenure by earning what was cynically known as a 'Tyburn Ticket'. This was intended as a reward for bringing a serious wrongdoer to justice who was hanged for his crimes. These 'Tyburn Tickets' were much sought after and could be bought and sold on the open market.

By Tudor times the duties of the magistrates included supervising and regulating inns and alehouses; maintaining bridges and roads; applying regulations on weights and measures; supervising the poor relief system; dealing with vagrants and controlling the houses of correction where the unemployed and others were put to work. The magistrates had a very important role to play in pre-industrial society but they tended to run things according to their own narrow class interests which meant that little sympathy was shown for the needs of the poorer sections of society. In 1744 Parliament decreed that only those who owned land worth a minimum of £100 a year could become magistrates. The system of voluntary, unpaid members of the landed class having a juridical function had evolved to meet the needs of a rural, feudal society but was impractical for a cosmopolitan place like London. The ever-changing population meant that it would not and could not accept the traditions of authority and deference that existed in the provinces. The time-honoured system of amateur JPs and constables simply could not cope with the enormous influx of people into the new industrial towns. Manchester's population, for example, was 6,000 in 1700 but rose to 50,000 in 1788, completely overwhelming the thin line of authority responsible for law and order. Most of London was situated in Middlesex, and it was here, not surprisingly, that appointments of stipendiary or paid magistrates were made for the first time in 1792.

Even in the seventeenth century increasing emphasis was placed on the services of volunteer associations of those citizens who believed that their property and livelihood were most threatened by criminal activity. These included the trained bands whose roll of honour included stopping the advance upon London of Charles I at Turnham Green during the Civil War. The eighteenth century witnessed the appearance of what we nowadays call vigilante bands and various groups who provided financial rewards for those who brought specified malefactors to justice.

Widely mocked were the watchmen who shuffled slowly around the streets of some of the country's towns and cities. Henry Fielding described them as, 'Being chosen out of those poor old decrepit people who are, from their want of bodily strength, rendered incapable of getting a livelihood by work. These men, armed only with a pole, which some of them are scarcely able to lift, are to secure the persons and houses of His Majesty's subjects from the attacks of gangs of young, bold, stout, desperate and well-armed villains.' Even the younger, stronger watchmen were usually open to being bribed. Watchmen were generally known as 'Charleys' because the force may have originated during the reign of Charles I and were regarded as a pushover. This can sometimes be taken literally because young men roistering drunkenly round the streets derived great pleasure from pushing over the small wooden sentry boxes into which the 'Charleys' usually retreated when it looked as if there might be serious trouble. They feature frequently in satirical art of the eighteenth and nineteenth centuries which presents a picture of stooped, gouty and asthmatic old men, hobbling round the streets at night, calling out the hour and the weather and by doing so instantly alerting any wrongdoers in the area to their presence. They were little use when it came to dealing with the increasingly ruthless gangs of well-organised criminals that were prominent at that time. During their patrols they scrupulously avoided those streets, alleys and lanes where crimes were most likely to be committed. As John Pearson said in *The London Charleys of the 18th Century; or Half-past Twelve O'clock, and a Very Cloudy Sort of a Morning*, published in 1827, '. . . the thieves are out in all weathers, and the more it rains, the more it blows, the more it hails, and the more it snows, the more the Charley will stick hard and fast to his box . . .'.[1] With all their very obvious limitations it seems remarkable that tentative proposals to replace them by a regular force of efficient paid policemen led to a sudden upsurge of affection and support for the fragile thin line they offered between stability and chaos.

As the eighteenth century progressed, increasingly widespread concerns began to be expressed about crime and disorder. In the absence of reliable quantifiable evidence it is difficult for historians to establish whether there really was a dramatic rise in the volume and nature of crime which is suggested by contemporary commentators. Court records certainly suggest increasing levels of theft and rioting. Evidence of the desperation in which street crime thrived was the 'mania' for gin-drinking which afflicted London in the first half of the eighteenth century. In 1725 it was estimated that 6,000 premises in London were selling gin, much of which was adulterated and highly poisonous. Gin attracted no excise from the Government and was therefore extremely cheap. London was a filthy, pestilential place in which life was brutish and short and gin presented a quick means whereby its most downtrodden and desperate citizens could escape from their misery. Many of them were more-or-less permanently drunk and would turn to robbery or prostitution to obtain the few pennies that were needed to buy enough gin to get dead drunk once again. Addiction to gin undermined the will to work or do anything positive. Physicians reckoned that many thousands of Londoners lived on gin alone and that gin was the cause of many premature deaths as well as untold hardship, violence, crime and despair.

The Gordon Riots in London in 1780 started as anti-Catholic demonstrations but soon degenerated into random plunder and destruction, etching themselves into the popular consciousness for the next sixty years. For several days the mob had acted with almost complete impunity while the authorities stood by seemingly powerless to make an effective intervention. In the event, soldiers and forces of armed civilians, such as the London Military Association, played a critical role in restoring order, but not before 450 people had been killed or seriously injured. This and their general perceptions led the upper and middle classes to agree that crime and social disorder were becoming acute problems requiring urgent action. However, there was little consensus about what measures should be taken or how they should be financed. Understandably, these concerns were expressed most forcibly regarding the situation in London. In the eighteenth century it experienced an enormous commercial and industrial boom and its population and geographical extent expanded with unprecedented speed. Despite the increasing overall affluence of the capital, there were many notorious 'rookeries'. These were squalid slums consisting of labyrinthine, noisome, unlit alleys, courts and narrow streets harbouring untold numbers of people who obtained their living largely or exclusively from the proceeds of criminal or illegal activity.

The problems of maintaining law and order resulted in the evolution of two types of widely criticised functionary, the trading justice and the thief-taker. The former were professional magistrates who made a living from the fees payable for their duties, an example in literature being 'Justice Thrasher' from Henry Fielding's novel *Amelia*, published in 1751. Thief-takers were attracted by the rewards offered to those bringing certain types of offender to justice and were effectively professional bounty hunters. Thief-takers acted in a freelance capacity but would also investigate robberies on behalf of the victims and charge them a commission for any stolen property that they recovered. The most notorious of these was Jonathan Wild, who is examined in Chapter Fourteen. He was a master criminal who controlled many gangs of London street robbers, receiving property they stole and restoring it to its owners for a fee. He was executed in 1725.

It was a trading justice, Sir Thomas De Veil, who made Bow Street magistrates' office a centre for the administration of justice in the Westminster district of London. De Veil was an interesting character with a real zest for life. Apart from enriching himself with his judicial fees, his main interest in life was sex. He married four times and these marriages produced no fewer than twenty-five children. His legal duties provided him with many opportunities for pursuing women which he did with single-minded determination. At Bow Street he maintained a private chamber to which he conducted an unending stream of women, most of whom gave themselves to him because they had got into scrapes that De Veil was prepared to overlook if they made it worth his while. He may have been sexually rapacious but for all that he revealed great courage in bringing many of London's most dangerous criminals to justice.

In 1749, after De Veil had died, the energetic Henry Fielding took over at Bow Street and following him his half-brother Sir John. Between them they launched the first systematic attack on London's criminal world. They took a more holistic view of their mission than De Veil had done, realising that prevention was at least as important as the cure of crime and that crime could not be prevented unless some attempt was made to understand its causes. In 1751 the elder Fielding published his 'Inquiry into the Causes of the Late Increase in Robbery' which contained perceptive insights into the nature and causes of crime and telling criticisms of the system of administering justice. He was convinced that gambling and gin-drinking were major contributory factors because those who were addicted needed to steal to finance their habits. Henry Fielding inherited a force of eighty constables and soon decided that only six had the necessary qualities. He also recommended that the reward for information leading to the conviction of highwaymen should be increased to £100.

In 1754 Henry died and was succeeded by John, widely known as the 'Blind Beak', who compensated for his total lack of sight with his uncanny hearing. He presided over affairs at Bow Street for twenty-six years and it was said that he could recognise 3,000 villains by their voices alone. It was the Fieldings who set up the patrols that evolved into the famous Bow Street Runners, who were professional thief-takers paid by results and whose services were open to hire by any who could afford them. Both Fieldings had extensive underworld contacts and these enabled them to get information quickly when crimes were committed and to gain an accurate idea of who had perpetrated them.

In the 1790s horse patrols were organised from Bow Street to watch the main roads into and out of London from evening until midnight, and these undoubtedly had the effect of restricting the activities of highway robbers. Other measures aimed at controlling highwaymen inaugurated by John Fielding were the circulation of printed handbills to stable-keepers which gave details of known highwaymen and their horses, and also the provision of armed guards on stagecoaches at times when highwaymen were known to be at large. These guards were recruited from retired cavalry soldiers and their inflexible methods meant that observant criminals were able to predict exactly where the patrols would be at any particular time. One highwayman, when captured, was found to be in possession of a complete roster of their patrols. Overall, however, they were successful enough to encourage the Government to provide some financial help. Bow Street was not popular with the criminal fraternity but the relative success of these early initiatives helped to create a climate of opinion that assisted Sir Robert Peel when, in April 1829, he presented his bill for a Metropolitan Police Force to Parliament. Another of Sir John Fielding's enterprises was the publication of a crime journal that circulated nationwide entitled 'Hue and Cry'. This made life increasingly difficult for those who carried out highway and street robberies and needed to find buyers for the articles they stole because it collated lists and descriptions of stolen items and also details of those who were wanted for questioning in connection with unsolved criminal offences.

In 1798 a group of shipping owners asked a leading London magistrate, Patrick Colquhoun, for advice on what measures to take in order to counter the massive, highly organised pilfering from ships that was taking place in and around the Pool of London. On his advice a marine police force was established in 1798 and in 1800 the Government stepped in and took the force over, calling it the Thames River Police. It was a well-disciplined force of regular officers not dependent for their livelihood on freelance activities and they quickly proved their worth. The Thames River Police are of key importance in the history of British crime because they were effectively the first open professional police force.

Various attempts were made to force Parliament to take action on the issue of the creation of a police force but they failed for a number of reasons. Proposals for a regular police force were likened to threatening Britain with the kind of notorious political police spy network that was familiar in France. It was argued that this would be inimical to the much vaunted if mainly illusory political liberties of the English subject. In 1811 two families were brutally killed on the Ratcliffe Highway in London's East End. The shock that these atrocities evoked sharply focussed attention on the lawlessness that was so rife in that cosmopolitan part of the capital and as Leon Radzinowicz said, 'Never before, not even after the Gordon Riots which brought the capital so close to total destruction, and gave so striking an illustration of the failings of the justices and parish constables, did the public express so vigorous and persistent a condemnation of the traditional machinery for keeping the peace.'[2] A select committee was established to consider what could be done to prevent similar crimes being committed. A member of the House of Lords, however, wrote at the time that as far as he was concerned the murder of half a dozen people every few years on the Ratcliffe Highway was preferable to the use of the police intimidation introduced in France at the height of the Jacobin Terror and associated with the dreaded name of Joseph Fouché, the Minister of Police. This noble peer was not, of course, an inhabitant of the East End.

The actual word 'police' was not to be found in English usage before 1714 and the ideological climate into which a visible and official body of law-enforcers, effectively paid for from taxes, could fit simply did not exist in the eighteenth century. However, two highly covert police forces were already operating. The King's Messengers kept an eye on 'subversive' movements, while the Press Messengers investigated publishers of seditious literature. In reality a secret service had long been established and extensive use was made of networks of spies and *agents provocateurs*. Nevertheless, as far as public pronouncements were concerned, this was the age of *laissez-faire*. Although the volume of goods and money being stolen every year was a matter of concern, it was argued that any resources made available to fight crime would be best spent offering rewards to individuals to seek out, inform on and capture known offenders. The provision of incentives to informants, often with accompanying free pardons, and the encouragement of the thief-takers, maybe criminals themselves, were the main solutions to the problem of crime detection in the eighteenth century. It was to take more than just a few murders, no matter how ferocious, to convince Parliament that a professional, visible police force was needed.

Earlier, in 1692, bounties had been made official when a general Act offered a reward of £40 for the conviction of a highwayman. Additionally, a free pardon where appropriate was available for the informer who also enjoyed the bonus of the highwayman's horse, weapons and money, unless they were known to have been stolen. The Government practice of offering rewards was followed by similar inducements from insurance companies, businesses and private individuals. Common informers and bounty hunters have always been loathed but in the early eighteenth and nineteenth centuries the conditions existed in which they could thrive. An informer needed a thorough knowledge of national law and also of local by-laws and could attract rewards varying from sums of 50s to over £150. For the really unscrupulous informer there were also lucrative opportunities for blackmail. Usually the common informer operated on a small scale and his victims were often petty offenders. More formidable and more feared were the professional thief-takers or bounty hunters. The opinion in Government circles in the eighteenth century was that the motivation for human behaviour was primarily self-interest and people, it was believed, were fundamentally greedy. Private enterprise in apprehending criminals and bringing them to justice and terror through exemplary punishment was believed to be the best way to control what was seen as the growing problem of crime. Evidence of concern about rising crime and the use of self-help in the absence of Government action was seen in the establishment of what can best be described as vigilante groups. In 1786, in Manchester for example, an Association of Proprietors had been set up to patrol the business premises of its members at night. In 1788 another local organisation, the Society for the Prosecution of Felons and the Receivers of Stolen Goods, was proud to declare that the prosecutions it had initiated the previous year had led to thirteen transportations, seven imprisonments and five whippings.

In 1795 Patrick Colquhoun's 'A Treatise on the Police of the Metropolis' was published. He was convinced that the overall decline of religious observance and the general decay of morals, most of all among the poor, were contributing to a serious increase in the amount of crime. He did not believe, however, that this could be cured by the simple introduction of increasingly draconian punishments. His answer was a police force totally independent of the judiciary and designed to prevent and detect crimes. He backed his argument with a mass of statistical evidence, which even in its raw state highlighted the scale of the problem facing the city of London. Each year £2 million was lost in the city simply through theft, while 115,000 people supported themselves through criminal, illegal or immoral activity of various sorts. Although too much reliance should not be placed on Colquhoun's statistics, this does not detract from his forcible argument in favour of the establishment of a police force. He went on to advocate the compulsory inspection of drinking places and the close supervision of prostitutes, gypsies, itinerant ballad sellers and others whose activities were seen as immoral or subversive. He advocated that severe punitive measures be taken against receivers because he argued that without them much of the activity of highway and street robbers would have been impossible. His ideas met with strong criticism from those who objected to the idea of snoopers and secret police, while others argued that he was attacking the symptoms of crime rather than its root causes. Colquhoun has an important place in the history of criminal theory because he was the first prominent person to seek explanations for criminality in material factors rather than metaphysical theories about morals, temptations and original sin.

Once the initial furore surrounding the Ratcliffe Highway murders had dissipated the mood changed to complacency and no political leader was prepared to urge the establishment of a permanent police force with effective financial support from the public purse. However, events soon overtook this attitude. The period from the end of the Napoleonic Wars to the 1840s saw unprecedented economic turmoil and political unrest which undoubtedly terrified the ruling class of the time, who saw subversion and possible revolutions everywhere. It can now be seen that these events reflected a temporary and unique conjuncture of socio-economic factors. They included the Luddite Riots of 1811, the Corn Law Riots of 1815, the 'Blanketeer' March and Riots of 1817, the 'Peterloo Massacre' in Manchester in 1819 and fierce outbreaks of rioting in many corners of the country, both urban and rural. Against these much use was made by the authorities of the hated yeomanry who were perceived as being dominated by well-to-do factory owners and industrialists and their sons, all eager for a scrap with the lower orders and starting off with an unfair advantage because they were mounted. Their mere presence at flashpoints, let alone the role they played and seemed so much to relish, was therefore highly provocative. Some political leaders wanted to develop increasingly coercive and repressive measures to crush the spirit of revolt for once and all. Others argued for a more gentle approach.

In 1820 investigations by Government spies revealed the Cato Street Conspiracy, the brainchild of the confused but fanatical Arthur Thistlewood. His plan was to assassinate the Cabinet, destroy the institutions of the City of London such as the Mansion House and the Bank of England, set fire to the city and then establish himself as dictator. He and his fellow conspirators learned that the entire Cabinet would be dining at the house of Lord Harrowby in Grosvenor Square in London's West End on 23 February 1820. They decided to attack them with knives, pistols and hand grenades. The ministers were to be slaughtered there and then but the heads of Lords Sidmouth and Castlereagh, the main proponents of increasingly repressive measures, were to be removed and taken away. This preposterous scheme failed because spies easily infiltrated the ranks of the conspirators. The historical importance of the Cato Street Conspiracy was that it concentrated the minds of the politicians. Some, such as Sidmouth, thought it vindicated more coercive measures. Shortly after the Cato Street affair, there was a further shock to the Government's sense of security. A small number of guardsmen mutinied when ordered into action against a mob that was attacking the houses of several prominent and unpopular ministers in London. The combination of the Cato Street Conspiracy and this uprising convinced one Cabinet member, the influential Duke of Wellington, that London urgently needed a new and very different kind of security force.

In January 1822, Sidmouth was persuaded to retire and the Prime Minister Lord Liverpool inspirationally replaced him as Home Secretary with Robert Peel. It was known that Peel favoured the idea of a thorough overhaul of the criminal law and the establishment of a centrally controlled police force. Peel faced a delicate situation because there were many MPs who were not yet convinced of the need for a police force. At first he shrewdly concentrated on the less controversial matter of reform of the criminal law and he carefully used this issue to develop his credibility and his allies. Few could argue with him about the need for action when he revealed that although the population had increased by 15½ per cent between 1821 and 1828, crime had increased by over 40 per cent. He was a master of the art of marshalling facts and presenting them in a persuasive way and he systematically built up his case for what he described as 'a gradual reformation' rather than by advocating root-and-branch change. Tactically it was a wise move to get the Duke of Wellington to introduce the Metropolitan Police Bill into Parliament via the House of Lords. The Bill met with little opposition and became law in 1829.

The resultant 'Bobbies', or 'Peelers', checked the apparent headlong growth of crime in London. Their duties were restricted entirely to the city at first and they were the first English policemen employed full-time on a regular wage which obviated bounty-hunting and the opportunities for crime and corruption that went with it. The very high turnover in the first few years was indicative of the stresses involved in establishing this pioneer force in what was the hub of Britain's criminal activity. The early 'Peelers' seemed to think that arrests were what policing was about and as a result they zealously rounded up drunkards, beggars and prostitutes in large numbers for various street offences because such action seemed to bring quick results. While this did not immediately make the streets of London a safer place, it is likely that their visible presence deterred street robbers. However, this did not mean that these offenders disappeared, and many street thieves and other criminals simply moved out of London to provincial towns which they regarded as providing easier and safer conditions for their activities. With some reluctance local authorities in the provinces set about establishing police forces of their own, modelled largely on the London example. Their slowness in doing so led the Government to intervene and pass the County and Borough Police Act in 1856 by which it became mandatory for counties and boroughs to set up police forces in the areas over which they had control.

Claude Duval holds up a coach, painting by W.P. Frith. This picture with the handsome, courteous and gallant highwayman, the fearful yet fascinated damsel and the dance in the moonlight encapsulates the romance that has attached itself to the activities of many highwaymen. The everyday reality was very different.

A satirical drawing by Rowlandson showing a 'Charley' or watchman going about his duties, and who is either studiously ignoring or incapable of seeing the burglary taking place behind him.

Two gentlemen are held up at gun point by a smock-wearing highwayman who discharges his pistols and frightens more than just the horses.

'Blind Beak' – Sir John Fielding, the Bow Street magistrate.

A plaque at Marble Arch, London, marking the site of the Tyburn Tree, although the exact position is disputed.

A public execution outside Newgate Prison in London, 1809. The penalty for those convicted of highway robbery was public hanging, and these occasions were immensely popular spectacles. This picture, however, does not emphasise the densely packed, voyeuristic crowds that were attracted to such events to witness the dying agonies of the condemned felons.

TWELVE

Prisons and Punishment

A traditional responsibility of Britain's rulers has been the control of crime, the enforcing of the rule of law and the provision of justice. In the early nineteenth century it was considered that the most effective deterrent to the commission of crime was execution, transportation to labour camps in the country's nascent overseas colonies and corporal punishment. There was no concept of expensive long-term custodial sentences which while punishing might also rehabilitate the convicted criminal. Prisons were primarily for the housing of those about to be brought to trial, awaiting sentencing or due for execution or transportation. Execution itself was carried out publicly and was meant to have a deterrent effect on those who witnessed it. It was also intended to inflict pain before it brought about death.

A range of punishments short of death was introduced in the sixteenth century in an attempt to counteract a perceived explosion of crime. Those without obvious means of supporting themselves were seen as a pool of potential criminality and treated accordingly. Those described as 'vagabonds' of fourteen years of age or more rendered themselves liable to being whipped and branded on the gristle of the right ear unless they went into service for a year. Many offences were punished with 'carting' which involved men and women being stripped to the waist, tied to a cart's tail and whipped through the streets. At the same time there was a remarkable growth in the number of capital offences, many of which were encapsulated in the infamous Waltham Black Act of 1722. This was 'An Act for the more effectual punishing wicked and evil disposed Persons going armed in Disguise, and doing Injuries and Violences to the Persons and Properties of His Majesty's subjects, and for the more speedy bringing the Offenders to Justice', and no other piece of legislation has ever prescribed the death penalty for so many offences.

Hanging, drawing and quartering seems especially barbaric and was inflicted on those found guilty of treason. For this reason it is not a form of execution we associate with highwaymen but at least one died in this ignominious fashion. James Hind made a speciality of robbing those on the Parliamentary side in the English Civil War and was tried and executed for treason rather than simple robbery. He underwent the time-honoured procedure whereby the condemned man was dragged on a hurdle to the place of execution and hanged briefly for a few minutes before being taken down. Then, while still alive, he was castrated, eviscerated and forced to watch while his intestines were burned in front of him. He was then beheaded and his torso was cut up into four pieces, which were treated with a preservative substance before being displayed in a prominent public place as a fearful warning to others. This appalling form of execution was dreaded not just for the pain involved but because of the strong belief then that a dead person could not enter the afterlife if his or her body was incomplete.

In the sixteenth and seventeenth centuries only about 50 offences had carried the death penalty but in the following 150 years capital crimes rose to well over 200. This led to the British penal system being widely referred to as the 'Bloody Code'. The increasing severity of the penal system was not accidental but was firmly rooted in the economic and social changes the country was undergoing. Britain was an advanced economy by the standards of the time and industry and commerce were growing very rapidly. Great wealth was being accumulated by many large landowners, merchants, bankers and industrialists and smaller amounts by the middle classes, and they all wanted their riches to be protected. At the same time an enormous increase in population in the eighteenth century created a host of problems pressing down on the poor, both in town and country, because of the absence of an infrastructure of social and other services to support them through a period of immense revolutionary change. This meant that society in the period 1700 to 1850 was essentially unstable, as governments attempted to handle a host of new and unforeseen problems with a legal and administrative apparatus that had evolved over centuries to serve the needs of a largely rural country.

The perception of the rich was that there was a threatening large-scale increase in crime and a decline in deference among the lower orders. The only way to meet rising criminality was by institutionalising further state brutality and violence and terrifying the population into observing the law. Public hangings were thought to provide an object lesson and a deterrent to those considering a career in crime. In the absence of effective policing, 'exemplary punishment' was used. This recognised that statistically the chances of an offender being apprehended were small and so it cruelly and callously made an example of those who were caught in an attempt to deter others. It did not work. In practice judges often used their discretion to mitigate the harshest provisions of the law, while juries found ways to reduce the gravity of the offences with which those who appeared in court were being charged. Execution for theft, despite it being a capital offence, was rare by the late eighteenth century, unless there were aggravating circumstances such as armed robbery or robbery by a gang.

The Rule of Law attempted to legitimate the 'Bloody Code' as a form of social control by developing the concept that all were equal before the law, that the law was an impartial arbiter operating without favour for the benefit of all citizens. This was the response of the ruling class in a now largely secular society to the loss of the social cement once provided by religion and the hierarchy of authority and control that went with it. It is unlikely that the common folk were fooled by such a stratagem. Anatole France, the

French writer, summed it up succinctly in 1894: 'The majestic egalitarianism of the law, which forbids rich and poor alike to sleep under bridges, to beg in the streets, and to steal bread.'

Highwaymen offended against the laws of property and the prison most associated with them is undoubtedly Newgate. This was a very old establishment and certainly in existence in 1189 because it is mentioned in a pipe roll of that date. It was the prison for the county of Middlesex as well as the City of London and jointly controlled by the sheriffs of those areas, who appointed its keeper. It acquired an evil reputation and in 1334 an official enquiry found that: 'Prisoners detained on minor charges were cast into deep dungeons, and there associated with the worst criminals. All were alike threatened, many tortured, till they yielded to the keeper's extortions . . .' In 1381 Newgate was extensively damaged by Wat Tyler's forces in the Peasants' Revolt but continued to be a focus of fear and repulsion. Damaged in the Great Fire of London in 1666, it was repaired and went on to house a number of highwaymen and other robbers before their execution at Tyburn.

In 1770 a programme of rebuilding commenced at Newgate which involved demolition of much of the existing structure, but the work was not completed before there was another attack on this hated edifice during the anti-Catholic Gordon Riots of 1780. The Suffolk poet George Crabbe (1754–1832) described this assault in his journal: 'I went close to it, and never saw anything so dreadful. The prison was a remarkably strong building; but determined to force it, they broke the gates with crows and other instruments . . . They broke the roof and tore away the rafters, and having got ladders, descended. Not Orpheus himself had more courage or better luck. Flames all around them . . . The prisoners escaped. I stood and saw about twelve women and eight men ascend from their confinement to the open air, and they were conducted through the streets in their chains. Three of these were to be hanged on Friday.' The ravening mob broke into Langdale's gin distillery close to Newgate at the junction of Fetter Lane and Holborn and witnesses described men, women and children lying face downwards and literally lapping up raw gin that had poured out of broken stills on to the street. Later, the mob ignited a vat of gin containing about 120,000 gallons and this disappeared in a column of fire that could be seen 30 miles away. The damage was quickly repaired and by 1783 Newgate was again open for business. Its first celebrity prisoner was the notorious Lord George Gordon who, despite having earlier orchestrated the anti-Catholic riots, subsequently converted to the Jewish faith. He was a prisoner at Newgate from 1787 to 1793, when he died within the precincts.

Newgate remained dark, ill ventilated and pestilential until well after the last highwaymen had passed through its portals. The stench of Newgate was such that pedestrians passing the prison often held their noses. Male prisoners often showed their contempt by urinating on them from the top floors of the building. Gin and beer were produced on the premises. In 1813, on the debtors' side, which was built to house 100 inmates, there were no fewer than 340 prisoners. In the female felons' ward, designed to house just 60 prisoners, 120 poor souls whiled away their miserable time. The women who were awaiting execution in Newgate were placed in a garret on the top floor into which they were allowed to lure as many men as possible for the purpose of sexual intercourse. If they became pregnant they could 'plead their bellies' and obtain a reprieve from the gallows. In 1902 Newgate was demolished and the Central Criminal Court or 'Old Bailey' was erected on the site soon after.

A prominent figure at Newgate was the Ordinary or chaplain. Superficially, his job appeared highly unrewarding and was sometimes hazardous. Apart from the fact that Newgate housed the dregs of society, it stank and was often ravaged by lethal fevers. Also, he personally had much to put up with from the inmates. However, there was never any difficulty in filling the position as there were many perks that went with it. As well as the salary and a rent-free house and various legacies, the Ordinary enjoyed a lucrative unofficial income from publishing and selling the condemned prisoners' last confessions. Sales of these were proportionate to the notoriety of the condemned prisoner and the sensationalism and graphic details provided. The Ordinary knew this and when necessary simply invented suitably lurid material. Actually, 'invention' is precisely the word that comes to mind because it was necessary to write up the 'last confession' and get it printed and distributed several days before to ensure that it would be available on the day of the execution. This meant that what was sold to the prurient crowds who flocked to watch the execution was extremely unlikely to be the actual last confession. Many of those who were condemned to be executed resolutely refused to make any confession at all, but this did not prevent the Ordinary from going ahead and producing the expected broadsheet, complete with a 'confession'.

Sometimes a prisoner 'stood mute', as the law tersely put it. This meant refusing to plead and could only be for two reasons: either the prisoner was dumb or he was awkward. If it were ascertained that the prisoner could not speak, he would be considered to be pleading not guilty. However, few things irked the authorities more than a prisoner they thought was wilfully unco-operative and who would not enter a plea when charged. If such a prisoner was in Newgate he was likely to be taken to the sinister Press Yard. Here he would make the acquaintance of the dreaded *'peine forte et dure'*, more usually known as 'the Press'. It involved the prisoner being stripped naked and laid flat upon his back. A board was placed on his chest and weights put on it. Frequently the weights amounted initially to 350 lb and with such a weight on their chests most prisoners quickly found their voices and hastened to enter a plea.

William Spiggot, arrested for highway robbery in 1720, adamantly refused to enter a plea. He was a fairly nondescript highwayman but his fortitude at this late stage of his career has to be admired. He most vociferously declared that he was going to stand mute and the authorities consigned him to the Press Yard. Spiggot knew the law but he was a brave man and he was prepared to die under the Press. The law decreed that if he pleaded guilty and was found guilty then all his property would be forfeited to the Crown. If he actually pleaded not guilty and was found guilty, the result would be the same. If he did not plead at all, his property could not be confiscated. Spiggot knew perfectly well that if he entered a plea, the court would find him guilty. It was his family that he was concerned about; he did not want them left destitute. Unfortunately for Spiggot, while he coped with 350 lb on his chest, after half an hour they added another 50 lb and his endurance gave way. He pleaded guilty. '*Peine forte et dure*' was abolished in 1772, by which time less credence was being given to confessions extracted under coercion and more to gathering and presenting convincing evidence.

A particularly notorious prisoner awaiting execution could prove a money-spinner for the gaolers. They unashamedly charged visitors either to view the prisoner from a distance or for a higher fee to approach and chat with him or her. Valentine Carrick got rather fed up with gaping voyeurs during his last few days in the condemned cell and he called out to them, 'Good folks, you pay for seeing me now, but if you had suspended your curiosity till I went to Tyburn, you might have seen me for nothing.' Well-liked rogues often found that they hardly had a moment to themselves during their last few days. Those who were of a sociable nature seem to have enjoyed the attention. The highwayman 'Sixteen String Jack' revelled in the limelight and entertained numbers of women for 'dinner' on the last few evenings before his execution. Not all prisoners were able to maintain their composure to the last. While William Hawke, also known as the 'Flying Highwayman', spent his last night rather incongruously praying and singing psalms, a companion due to hang with him was trembling like an aspen leaf and had to be helped up into the cart. The highwayman John Ashton totally lost his reason under the pressure of awaiting his execution and once on the scaffold at Newgate began telling the crowd that he was Lord Wellington.

On the morning of the execution, the condemned prisoner was unshackled and had his elbows pinned back leaving his hands free. Those prisoners thought to be a particular security risk were handcuffed. A noose was hung about the neck. The condemned prisoner left Newgate on a horse-drawn cart at 10 in the morning to travel the 3 miles to Tyburn, the route being Snow Hill, High Holborn, St Giles's and along what was then called Oxford Road. Well-off prisoners sometimes rode in their own conveyances. Soon after leaving Newgate the cart stopped outside St Sepulchre's so that the condemned prisoner could have the benefit of hearing the bellman's final proclamation and receiving a floral wreath. On the ride to Tyburn the prisoner had the company of the hangman and the Ordinary and usually sat on his personal coffin. They were preceded by the City Marshal on his horse and the Under-Sheriff with several mounted peace officers. Bringing up the rear were men on foot with pikes and halberds. When there were multiple executions there was a rule of precedence. The first two rows in the cart, the place of honour, went to those who had robbed the mail and to highwaymen. Those who were determined to make an impression often dressed in their best and carried themselves with a studied air of nonchalance. Others preferred a show of defiance. The spectators warmed to such prisoners but could not stand a cringing, cravenly display of fear when they would howl derisively and make the prisoner's last moments even more painful. They loved bravado and enjoyed the highwayman Jerry Abershaw who swaggered up to the scaffold with a red rose between his teeth after hastily discarding his boots. He did this because he suddenly recalled that his mother had warned him that if he did not give up his criminal ways, he would die with his boots on.

It was common practice for the entourage to stop at one or more alehouses on the way to Tyburn where the prisoner alighted with the Ordinary and guards to enjoy a complementary drink. This represented sound business sense by the publican because the prisoner would be followed in by a crowd eager to make his acquaintance or to wish him well personally. It was not unknown for a condemned prisoner to be totally drunk by the time he arrived at Tyburn. This custom certainly seems strange to us today but it gave rise to Dean Swift's famous piece of satirical verse:

GOING TO BE HANGED, 1727

As clever Tom Clinch, while the rabble was bawling,
Rode stately through Holborn to die in his calling,
He stopt at the George for a bottle of sack,
And promised to pay for it when he came back.
His waistcoat and stockings and breeches were white;
His cap had a new cherry ribbon to tie't
The maids to the doors and the balconies ran,
And said, 'Lack-a-day, he's a proper young man!'
But, as from the windows the ladies he spied,
Like a beau in the box, he bow'd low on each side!
And when his last speech the loud hawkers did cry,
He swore from the cart, 'It's all a damn'd lie!'
The hangman for pardon fell down on his knee;
Tom gave him a kick in the guts for his fee;
Then said, 'I must speak to the people a little,
But I'll see you all damned before I will whittle! . . .'

The site of Tyburn was close to the present Marble Arch. The first recorded execution was as early as 1196. For many centuries other locations in London used for hanging included Cornhill and Smithfield, where the highwayman John Cottington was hanged in 1656. The original gallows at Tyburn consisted simply of two poles with a crossbeam but by the sixteenth century this accommodation had become insufficient to meet the demand and a more substantial apparatus was erected. This allowed for the hanging of no fewer than twenty-four miscreants simultaneously. It lasted until 1759 when the 'Triple Tree', as it was known, was removed because it was an obstacle to traffic. After that a moveable gallows was used, which was kept at Newgate and erected at Tyburn every time it was needed. This gallows contained a trapdoor through which the victim dropped. The first to experience the new device was the hated Earl Ferrers who chose this method rather than the beheading that was more normal for peers of the realm. The gallows at Tyburn was known as the 'Tyburn Tree' or 'Jack Ketch's Tree' after the singularly incompetent public hangman who served there from 1663 to 1686. After his death, 'Jack Ketch' became the generic name for all hangmen. The popularity of public hangings with everyone except the condemned prisoner and perhaps his closest relatives and friends meant that a grandstand was erected in 1729. Seats in the grandstands that became known as 'Mother Proctor's Pew' were expensive, but gave those who could pay a particularly fine view of the proceedings. Mother Proctor was its owner and she never made a wiser investment.

Occasionally a hangman would turn up for work clearly the worse for drink. In 1738 the hangman at Tyburn was so confused that, to roars of approval from the crowd, he not only slipped nooses over the heads of the two robbers scheduled to be turned off that day, but also did the same for the Ordinary. Only with some difficulty was he persuaded not to hang him.

Eight 'hanging days' were set aside each year for executions at Tyburn and these were made into public holidays and referred to as Tyburn Fair. London was *en fête* and huge crowds lined the route from Newgate especially if one or more of the condemned prisoners was popular and likely to provide good entertainment. They would be bombarded with flowers and nosegays. The crowds would also turn out in large numbers to hurl missiles such as mud, stones, excrement and dead cats and dogs and to jeer at someone whose crimes they disapproved of. Jack Sheppard proved to be a major attraction and an estimated 100,000 spectators wished him well as he made his way to Tyburn on his last triumphal progress. Others that drew large crowds included 'Sixteen String Jack' and James

Maclaine in 1774 and 1750 respectively, although, as mentioned elsewhere, Maclaine gave poor value for money. On one unforgettable occasion, the procession was nearing Tyburn when the hangman, William Marvell, was arrested and carried away under escort. The crowd loved this but their elation turned to a sense of anti-climax and then anger when the three men due to be hanged were taken back to Newgate.

In early days the condemned prisoner had to mount a ladder with a rope tied around his neck and then jump off the ladder into space. This system was superseded by the prisoner being placed on a horse-drawn cart that was suddenly drawn forward leaving him dangling in mid-air. His friends and relations might then rush forward to pull on his legs to speed his despatch. The dead prisoner was supposed to be left to hang for half an hour. The crowd seemed inured to the indignity of hanging, as a contemporary observer said, '. . . there is nothing in being hanged but a Wry neck, and a wet pair of Breeches'.[1] What they watched was horrible and many criminals took minutes to die. For every one who died bravely, there were far more who died expelling faeces and urine. The penis might become erect and ejaculate, so it is said, and the uterus would bleed. Sometimes the rope snapped or the scaffold collapsed.

Mysterious powers were credited to the corpse of a hanged convict. Even before the executed felon had stopped twitching, women would rush forward to place his hand on their cheeks, necks or breasts. Probably few things would be more likely to restore a male prisoner to instant life than the last of these. However, the women were not doing it for the man's benefit but for their own. A hanged man's touch was supposed to cure warts and other skin blemishes.

One of the perks of the hangman was to keep the clothes of his victims, which would often sell for a very good price especially if the deceased was notable. Therefore, it was bursting with an understandable sense of righteous indignation that the hangman argued with a female prisoner in the cart on her way to Tyburn. Her name was Hannah Dagoe and she proposed to take all her clothes off and throw them into the crowd. She started with her gloves and bonnet when the hangman tried to restrain her. However, Hannah was big and strong and holding him off with one hand she continued to divest herself of her garments, throwing them into the highly appreciative crowd. She almost managed to knock the hangman off the cart before she was restrained by the guards. When she mounted the scaffold she was absolutely naked. An even more unsavoury episode accompanied the hanging of the rapist John Briant in 1797. Here a brutal struggle took place between one group of his female relatives consisting of those who wanted to take the body away for burial and another band of women who wanted to strip the corpse to remove its clothing for its imagined therapeutic properties. It is difficult to say who won this heated fracas but it certainly was not the dignity of the deceased. His legs, arms and head were all ripped off.

It was common for relatives to claim the body of a hanged convict and to take it away after the prescribed half an hour. It was not unusual for attempts to be made to resuscitate the deceased. A bellows might be used to pump air and other vital substances into the lungs, the air passages and the spine might be pressed and massaged while hot vapours might be forced up the anus. Being restored to life in this way must have been a highly unpleasant experience.

Aversion to the idea of large crowds turning out to witness executions is a comparatively recent development. Dr Samuel Johnson (1709–84) can be regarded as a cultured intellectual and was aghast when in 1783 it was proposed to abolish public executions at Tyburn. He wrote to a friend that the whole purpose of a public hanging was precisely to draw the maximum possible number of spectators: 'The public liked it and the condemned man felt encouraged by it,' he declared. Johnson just lived to see the end of hangings at Tyburn on 7 November 1783 after which time the place of execution was switched to outside Newgate Prison itself.

The scaffold was not a permanent one and was erected during the night before an execution and then taken down. At least one condemned prisoner due to hang in the morning complained most bitterly that the banging, hammering and merry banter of the workmen had kept him awake all night at the very time when he felt he had never had greater need of a good night's undisturbed sleep.

Hangings outside Newgate continued to attract large crowds of the morbid, the curious, the criminal and the sadistic. Several large houses offered an excellent view of proceedings around the scaffold. These windows were rented by the rich who fortified themselves from hampers replete with delicacies such as cooked tongue, smoked hams, sandwiches and sherry, champagne and cigars. Less expensive titbits were hawked on the street below. These included pies of dubious provenance, sticky cakes, ginger beer and a variety of sweetmeats.

Hangings at Tyburn or Newgate were for crimes perpetrated in the City of London and the county of Middlesex and they have been covered at some length because there is more evidence about crime and punishment in London than anywhere else in the eighteenth century. Many other locations, such as county towns like York and Maidstone, which housed the assizes and were near busy roads, saw executions including those of highwaymen. In fact, over 70 per cent of executions in the early nineteenth century took place outside of London in the provinces.

From the middle of the eighteenth century, an increasing number of people began to question the morality and efficacy of England's Draconian penal system. The feeling was growing that public executions, a brutal example of institutionalised violence, no longer provided any deterrent. The whole event had assumed the nature of a carnival with condemned felons frequently basking in the adulation of the crowd while every opportunity was taken to mock the law and its officials. Charles Dickens when attending the execution of the murderer Courvoisier in 1840 described the event and said that in the audience he saw no emotion suitable to the occasion, '. . . No sorrow, no salutary terror, no abhorrence, no seriousness; nothing but ribaldry, debauchery, levity, drunkenness, and flaunting vice in fifty other shapes'.[2] Various enquiries and committees investigated the issue and they began to compile evidence. This is an excerpt from the proceedings of one such committee:

> What effects are produced by such executions? – They merely come to see an execution of that kind as a spectacle; they go away again and waste their time; and many of the spectators commit crimes, as I have reason to suppose, before the night closes, after witnessing such a scene: nay, we had a boy brought in some time ago, who had only a few days before been out of Newgate; he was brought in for picking pockets under the gallows; and when I spoke to him upon the subject, and said, 'How could you do such a thing at such an awful moment?' He said, 'Sir, that was the best moment in the world, for everybody's eyes were up when the drop was falling'.[3]

Between 1756 and 1765 there were 329 persons convicted of criminal offences of whom 183 were executed, that is, about 50 per cent. Between 1795 and 1804 the ratio of those hanged to those convicted fell to about 17 per cent. The number capitally convicted continued to fall, as did the percentage actually executed.

Catastrophes such as that which accompanied the hanging in 1807 of the convicted murderers Haggerty and Holloway helped to strengthen opinion against public executions. They were to be executed outside Newgate and a huge crowd, estimated at 40,000, gathered and the sheer weight of numbers was such that panic broke out in the crowd. People at the front were being squashed by those behind straining to get a good view. One or two desperately trying to escape from the confusion may have slipped and fallen and others tumbled over them. It took an hour to secure some semblance of order from the ensuing chaos but by that time twenty-eight were dead and nearly seventy injured. Horrors of this sort were by no means restricted to London, and in August 1844 at least a dozen people were trampled or crushed to death at a hanging in Nottingham. The Mayor of Nottingham wrote to the Home Office: 'It is right that I should immediately inform you of a most calamitous occurrence which has taken place today . . . The case has excited extreme interest, and a vast crowd was assembled early in the morning to see the execution . . . It was no sooner over than a tremendous rush of the multitude was made from the Scaffold down the High Pavement Street. A confusion excited by mischievous persons throwing hats and shoes about originated the general desire to escape from the overpowering pressure. Numbers of persons were thrown down, run over and trodden upon. The shrieks and cries of the sufferers are beyond description.'[4]

By the middle of the nineteenth century it was felt that the didactic and deterrent effects of hangings had more or less evaporated. They were now little more than a form of popular entertainment, degrading to the spectators and debasing the gravity of the law. Additionally, they attracted large crowds of unruly people who were seen as posing a threat to law and order. It came as no surprise that the last public hanging in Britain was staged in 1868, outside Newgate on 26 May.

THIRTEEN

Street Robbery

For hundreds of years many religious houses had offered sanctuary or immunity from arrest to fugitives from the law. This ecclesiastical privilege was largely swept away in Tudor times but 'sanctuaries' of another sort remained in London. These were the 'rookeries' which were effectively criminal enclaves whose inhabitants mostly lived by begging and by theft, robbery and other criminal practices. Only the most foolhardy of strangers ever penetrated these places and they were visited by the authorities on rare occasions and then at great risk to themselves. Individuals or gangs of criminals simply melted away down the nearest forbidding passage where any pursuer would find every hand turned against him. In the sixteenth century the most notorious of these places was Whitefriars later renamed 'Alsatia', close to the Temple on the south side of Fleet Street. Its inhabitants claimed that it was outside the jurisdiction of officialdom and in practice this was so. It continued to provide a safe haven for the members of the underworld until the nineteenth century. Later on, other rookeries such as St Giles and the Southwark area on the South Bank played the same role, providing a secure base for criminals and all sorts of underworld creatures.

Although historians argue about the extent to which the dissolution of the monasteries was a cause, it cannot be denied that there was a large increase in the number of beggars throughout the kingdom and on the streets of London in particular during the sixteenth century. An estimate in 1517 put the number of

London's mendicants at about 1,000 but by 1594 the number had risen to more than 12,000. The perception is that during the same period there was a substantial increase in crime and therefore it was easy and convenient to link vagrancy with crime and to discredit all those who could or would not work. In fact, many vagrants had been physically stigmatised and were left with few options other than crime, begging or starvation. Draconian measures against beggars failed to stem their increasing numbers in London, and in Houndsditch, Smithfield and the Barbican unsavoury shanty towns sprang up, as they do today in cities in the developing world.

The practice developed of placing the indigent into three categories: orphans; the sick, feeble and aged; and 'sturdy vagabonds'. It was readily assumed that fit-looking men without obvious means of support were wilfully refusing to work and preferred to beg or indulge in crime. It was these 'sturdy vagabonds' who were seen as the real problem. The authorities in the City of London took over the old Bridewell Palace and converted it into a house of correction where it was hoped that a judicious mixture of whipping and forced labour would both punish them and instil the work ethic into all but the hardest cases. However, beggars and thieves continued their depredations unabated. Modes of operation were many and varied. There were, for example, beggars known as 'Abraham men' who pretended to be simple-minded while 'dummerers' feigned being deaf mutes. Constables did not deal gently with such people and there is a record of a constable tying up a dummerer, hoisting him high over a beam and then letting him hang there. The constable laconically remarked that this treatment effected a rapid cure, for the man was soon howling in agony and imploring to be taken down. 'Demanders for glimmer' and 'freshwater mariners' beseeched alms on the grounds that they had been ruined by fire and shipwreck respectively.

In Elizabethan London one of the hazards with which those on the streets had to contend with was the activity of the 'cony-catchers'. They walked the streets looking for a likely victim who would probably be a gullible stranger up from the country. A way would be found to engage him in a friendly chat and, pleased to have found someone to befriend him in the unknown city, the unwitting victim would be only too happy to step into a nearby tavern for a pot of ale. The tavern was likely to be a 'flash house' which combined the functions of a drinking place, a brothel and a place of resort for the local low-life where they planned their next villainy and shared out the spoils from earlier ones. Once the man was in there, he was unlikely to leave without having lost all his money and valuables. He might be cheated at cards or dice or be unable to resist the temptation when a whore was laid on for his delectation. In this case, it is likely that he would be robbed when *in flagrante delicto*. Then, finding himself penniless and once again alone, he would be left to ponder ruefully over the moral turpitude of London and its inhabitants.

Orphans were recruited into the underworld at a young age, often learning their skills in a bizarre parody of the modern concept that combines classroom education with work experience. There were 'academies' where they learned how to extract coins silently from the pockets of garments hung round with bells or to cut the strings attaching a purse to a belt without the victim sensing anything. Others learned the skills of attracting attention and sympathy as beggars. Even small children might be veterans of crime. One Thomas Miller received his first conviction in 1845 at the age of eight and by the time he was twelve he had been in prison five times and received two whippings. Many of the children responsible for a myriad of street offences were orphaned or abandoned and it is difficult to see what alternative they had to living by crime.

After Jonathan Wild's downfall in 1725, his criminal empire broke up. He was the master thief-taker and London's first underworld leader and his meticulous methods of organisation were copied by other underworld operators. In the 1750s one of these gangs is recorded as having members who specialised solely in 'cheating, thieving or robbing', meaning that they were cardsharpers, pickpockets or footpads. It also had administrative 'offices', its 'treasury' or fund of venture capital and its pool of peripheral gang members who were only too happy to act as false witnesses. Many of the gangs who operated in London from the mid-1700s to about 1800 were both formidable and fearsome. They brazenly ranged the streets in bands numbering twenty to thirty virtually immune from arrest, openly attacking passers-by and robbing them in broad daylight. Anyone foolhardy enough to try to fight back risked injury or death, while the constables and watchmen would usually turn a blind eye for fear of being set upon themselves. The authorities felt that the only way to combat rising crime was the already well-tried and unsuccessful one of increasing the number of capital offences and displaying the gory remains of highwaymen, footpads and others on gibbets in prominent public places in the hope that these would have a deterrent effect.

Among the most frightening street gangs were the 'Mohocks', whose activities are first recorded in 1712. They were young men from fashionable, well-off families who roamed the streets of London looking to create trouble. This sometimes took the form of robbery but was just as likely to start when they spied anyone who looked vulnerable or different. They might beat them with sticks, mutilate or stab them and on occasions they would place one of their victims in a barrel and roll them down a hill. One of their favourite tricks was to catch hold of an attractive young woman and force her to do a handstand in the street. In the days when women did not wear drawers, the humiliation that this involved can only be guessed at.

Pickpockets and shoplifters were regarded as among the more lowly members of criminal society, and the former were everywhere. A foreign visitor to London wrote: 'Pickpockets are legion. With extraordinary dexterity they will steal handkerchiefs, snuff-boxes, watches – in short, anything they can find in your pockets. Their profession is practised in the streets, in churches, at the play, and especially in the crowds.' This crime was committed by thieves of all ages but especially by young children who often used it as a stepping-stone to greater things in the world of crime. A small boy, Richard Oakey, was hanged for robbery in 1723. He was a cutpurse and would trip a woman up from behind and in the wink of an eye as she fell, he would have her purse. A variation of this trick was to seize a woman as a coach sped by on the pretext of saving her from being run down. The woman's first instinct might be gratitude towards her saviour which would swiftly turn to outrage when she realised she had been most skillfully robbed.

Many parts of London were dangerous to pass through even in daylight hours. Moorfields was nicknamed 'Sodomites Walk' because of the depredations of the youths and young men who seized older men and extorted money from them by threatening to take them before a magistrate and have them charged with 'unnatural' acts. 'Witnesses' were on hand to attest to any complaint. In that part of Smithfield known as 'Jack Ketch's Warren', an ingenious arrangement allowed refugees from the law to escape through an upstairs window of The Red Lion Inn on a sliding plank that would pass them over the Fleet Ditch to a house on the far side. Then the plank would be drawn in behind them. This area was notorious for its pickpocket and shoplifting 'academies'. The streets and myriads of entries, alleys and courtyards provided an almost perfect location for robbery. At certain times of the day traffic was almost at a standstill. Tempers were easily frayed and in the mêlée that followed it was all too easy for gangs of pickpockets to jostle people in the crowd and to rifle through their pockets in the ensuing confusion.

Everyone feared the activities of the vicious footpads. The crowded streets and the dingy alleys, courts and teeming rookeries of eighteenth- and nineteenth-century London provided the ideal location for their activities. Knowing that if caught they would almost certainly be hanged, they were prepared to kill their victims secure in the knowledge that 'dead men tell no tales'. The hazards encountered walking the streets of Georgian England did not just include highwaymen, footpads and the like, frightful though they may have been. They also involved running the gauntlet of constant importuning from prostitutes and supplications from legions of beggars, some of whom were extremely aggressive. To walk the streets of any town at this time was also to take a chance with refuse, excrement and other ordure heaved out of upstairs windows or tossed at random out of front doors.

Sometimes footpads, and they usually worked in gangs, specialised in quite sophisticated types of crime. In the 1720s a gang led by Obadiah Lemon developed 'the rattling lay', or robbery from coaches. They adapted a technique used by burglars which involved putting a fishing hook and line through a window and using it to snatch hats, wigs and scarves from travellers in carriages. The gang graduated to bushwhacking coaches and carriages when they ground to a halt in traffic. They would emerge suddenly from a dark alley and rush the vehicle, grabbing any trunks, boxes and other items they could and then immediately disappear down the same stygian passage into the rookeries, making pursuit virtually impossible. Growing bolder still, they would place an obstacle across the highway forcing a stagecoach to stop and when the coach driver alighted they would fire a couple of shots to terrify the passengers and then proceed to strip them of all their valuables. In the wink of an eye they were gone. These thieves were known as 'dragsmen' and from the 1830s found promising new hunting grounds around the big railway stations. Here large numbers of travellers gathered, often accompanied by copious amounts of luggage and with cabs and other conveyances moving here and there. Hackney cabmen had a dubious reputation and were often in league with the thieves.

New forms of technology are frequently exploited by enterprising criminals and it was so with railways, which resulted in new forms of highway robbery developing. Villains soon found it was possible to rob lone passengers in compartments in the early trains which ran without corridor connections or any form of alarm system. After four robbers had picked on a Swiss traveller on the London and North Western Railway and stripped him of his possessions, forcing him to risk life and limb by jumping out of the train while it was moving, an anxious correspondent wrote to one of the newspapers: 'Can nothing be done to bring back the good old days of Dick Turpin who was a brave and noble fellow compared with the cowardly brutes that infest our railways?' As early as 1853, David Stevenson, the Goods Manager of the same railway company wrote: 'Thieves are pilfering the goods from our wagons here to an impudent extent. We are at our wits' end to find out the blackguards. Not a night passes without wine hampers, silk parcels, drapers' boxes or provisions being robbed . . .' Villains invented many ingenious tricks. They might, for example, enter the guard's van of a train going from, say, Paddington to Oxford and deposit a worthless item of luggage marked for an intermediate station like Reading. They would then surreptitiously stick labels also marked 'Reading' to cover labels for 'Oxford' on any worthwhile-looking items of luggage. When Reading was reached they simply re-entered the guard's van and carried away those items they had identified earlier.

Even before the advent of the railways, the criminal fraternity had found new opportunities on the first horse-drawn omnibuses that started running in London in 1829. These were owned by George Shillibeer and ran from Paddington to the Bank. The service was not very successful and Shillibeer withdrew the vehicles, but omnibuses soon successfully entered service elsewhere in London, and by 1839 600 were operating and this rose to 1,300 in 1850. They provided excellent opportunities for pickpockets, who were invariably women. The fares were expensive at first and therefore the clientele well-to-do, which meant that pickpockets had much to gain from their method of travel. However, great care had to be exercised by robbers because of the difficulty of escaping from the vehicle once a theft had been discovered. The pickpockets were usually most interested in stealing coins because it was far more difficult to disprove ownership of these than a watch or a silk handkerchief, for example. The early vehicles were notorious for their poor springs and the sudden jerks and lurches helped to cover the actions of the thieves as they pressed against their victims. The conductors were known as 'cads' and often colluded with the pickpockets.

One of London's major highways has always been the River Thames. In the eighteenth and nineteenth centuries the river was alive with ships and smaller craft which conveyed merchandise of every sort, as well as passengers who usually found it quicker and sometimes safer to use the river when going about their business in the capital. Assaults on affluent travellers on the Thames by what were basically pirates occurred from time to time, although the main object of the riparian robbers was the cargoes of the ships being loaded and unloaded in the Pool of London. This theft was on a massive scale and was systematic and highly sophisticated. It was only the creation of the Thames River Police and the building of enclosed docks such as the West India Dock in 1802 and the East India Dock in 1806 that brought this form of highway robbery under some degree of control.

As ever, the poor preyed on each other. Footpads waited outside public houses for drunken men to leave because they were an easy target. They might simply knock them down and seize watches, wallets and other valuables or they might work with a woman posing as a prostitute when they would operate the 'buttock and twang'. This involved the woman luring the victim down a darkened alley with the offer of sexual services. As soon as he had dropped his breeches and could not defend himself easily, he would be attacked and robbed by the woman's accomplice. Footpads needed to be quiet and quick and they frequently used weapons that would temporarily incapacitate but not kill their victims. These might be short, thick cudgels, or a tube of canvas containing sand or a small piece of spherical shot, probably weighing 2 lb and enclosed in a stocking. In the middle of the eighteenth century footpad activity in London was so prevalent that well-armed robbers picked on individuals in places as busy as the Strand and Covent Garden, simply knocking them down and rifling through their pockets, sometimes in broad daylight. Footpads were especially active late in the evening when well-to-do people came out of the theatres. No footpad ever became a popular hero nor was there any sympathy for him or her when they were caught unless they had some extraordinary skill that aroused a degree of admiration. One such was 'Jumping Joe Lorrison', renowned for his dare-devil leaps into moving wagons in order to rob them, and another was Tom Gerrard, executed in 1711, who taught his dog to extract valuables from the pockets of passers-by.

Pickpockets frequently worked in small gangs. One would accost or bump into the victim, a second might carry out the actual robbery while the third kept a lookout or provided a diversion or obstruction if his fellows were discovered and chased. The street thieves of the highest calibre, the highly skilled adult pickpockets known as the 'swell mob', moved around widely in search of the richest pickings. They favoured places such as theatres, race meetings, public hangings and fairs and operated in well-co-ordinated gangs, relieving people in the crowd of items such as handkerchiefs, snuffboxes, watches, pocket books and banknotes. While they were the cream of street thieves, many drank to excess or took opiates and found that the speed and dexterity which they needed to remain at the top of their profession was compromised as a result.

'Gonophs' were run-of-the-mill pickpockets and street thieves. They would usually be found operating in the bustling streets close to the rookeries from whence they came and they bore out the inescapable truism that the poor largely stole from each other. They were opportunists who had no qualms about snatching a halfpenny from the grubby fingers of an urchin who had been sent by his mother to make some minor purchase at a nearby market stall. This type of robbery was known as the 'kinchin lay'. They also flocked to the environs of the railway stations, which were frequently in the less fashionable districts, while docks and markets also attracted them in substantial numbers. These all offered a location in which they could move about readily without exciting suspicion. The poorer districts contained most of the receivers' premises and possessed a subculture in which, despite the fact that villains preyed on each other and their neighbours, everyone would act together to confuse or obstruct police officers or others pursuing fugitives.

Because the law tended to deal so harshly with pickpockets using violence, those who had been robbed were sometimes reluctant to hand them over to the authorities, especially if what had been stolen was immediately recovered. Sometimes a good hiding would be administered there and then and the matter closed. However, no footpad or pickpocket could be sure of this. In 1826 George Catherall also known as 'Captain Slash' appeared in court at Northampton accused of having robbed a shoemaker at Boughton Green Fair of eleven half-crowns, one crown, one waistcoat, a neckerchief, a corkscrew and a few halfpennies. He was dishevelled and his head and hands were bound up with bandages. He had been beaten up when seized and among the injuries were a fracture of the skull, two broken ribs and broken bones in his hands. He was hanged.

What seems to be a surprisingly common form of street robbery was the stealing of laundry. Working class washerwomen would service the requirements of the better-off folk who lived in the relatively salubrious suburbs of London such as Camberwell, Earls Court or Camden Town. To do so it was necessary to transport cleaned and soiled items to and fro and this brought these women to the attention of small gangs, some of whom would restrain the victim while others grabbed the laundry basket and made off with it. Good items fetched worthwhile prices in the second-hand clothes markets. Girls were often involved in thieving in the street and one crime that seems to have been their speciality was 'skinning'. This involved luring a small but well-dressed child into some dark corner where it was stripped, naked if necessary, and the attacker would make off with its clothes. This offence was usually carried out in the winter because the child would have more clothes on. No thought was given to the wretched infant then having to make its way home through streets that might be cold and wet. Female clothing in the eighteenth and nineteenth centuries did not really aid its wearer's quick movement but it seems that women always excited less suspicion than men did if they loitered about. For this reason women frequently posed as shoppers and stole goods from market stalls and shops, many of which displayed as much as they could at the front in the open and on the pavement.

In the early 1860s, a wave of panic swept London because of the sudden proliferation of an old but fairly rare method of robbery known as 'garotting'. To be effective, the robbers had to work in a small gang and to employ speed and skill. The 'choker' seized the victim from behind and slipped a rope, cloth or simply a brawny arm around the victim's neck. He would then exert sufficient pressure to cause the victim to double up or even faint. While the victim was held in a steely grip the choker's partners would rifle his pockets. The garotting scare was a minor example of mass hysteria and it reached its peak in the summer of 1862. In July, an MP called Pilkington was robbed swiftly and silently while making his way through a well-lit and fashionable part of London from Parliament to his club. On the same night an eminent and venerable antiquarian was similarly attacked nearby. Those who read the more sensational magazines of the time were already being treated to hair-raising tales of thugee and other exotic forms of highway robbery in India. This added an element of spurious romance and mystery to these robberies and soon various people seeking the limelight were regaling the newspapers with entirely fictional accounts of how they had been assaulted by these stranglers of the night. Anti-garotting vigilante groups soon sprang up, and the mood of panic was whipped up by the newspapers. *The Times* declared the crime to be 'un-British' and expressed some surprise and not a little chagrin when those arrested for one of the early outbreaks turned out to be as British as *The Times* itself. The paper had been most gratified during an earlier scare in 1856 when some foreigners had been arrested for garotting. With xenophobia at fever pitch, *The Times* had urged that the 'Italian ruffians' who swaggered around with stilettoes in Whitechapel and Stepney should be instantly deported.

Neither did *Punch* magazine provide a measured response to the outbreak of garotting. Although it seemed to deplore these outrages, it made them into the theme for a sustained campaign of comical articles, songs and cartoons. This extract is from *Punch*, 6 December 1862.

> Come let us be merry and drink while we may,
> More Punch, Tom, and see that it's hotter,
> And hope going home we shan't meet on the way
> Sweet Sentiment's Pet, the Garotter . . .
>
> A gentleman's walking perchance with a crutch
> He'll suddenly stagger and totter;
> Don't think that the gentleman's taken too much
> He's unluckily met a garotter . . .
>
> There are but three ways to get out of his beat
> Turn coachman, or tiler, or yachter,
> For no one who walks on her Majesty's street
> Is safe from the scoundrel Garotter.

Such publications undoubtedly played a role in orchestrating a sense of fear and in advocating the creation of bands of anti-garotte vigilantes. The *Weekly Dispatch* made continual references to this theme and in December 1862 it declared: 'The manner in which anti-garotters armed to the teeth proceed along the streets at night, clinking their sword canes and ready to draw at a moment's notice, is calculated to strike terror into the breasts of others as well as those of the great enemy.'

The hysteria prevalent at this time had its effects in the courts and it is probably no coincidence that in 1863 more people were hanged for street robbery than at any time in the previous two decades. In the same year what was commonly known as the Garotting Act went through Parliament, which brought in flogging for convicted offenders, a punishment that was carried out with great rigour. To make it worse, the flogging was inflicted in instalments and even the most hardened of garotters quailed at the knees on being sentenced to receive this punishment. However, it had the desired effect and the garotting craze died out soon afterwards.

In Victorian England the most common experience of crime was probably to be the victim of a pickpocket. They infested public transport, the streets, meetings and gatherings of all sorts and places of entertainment. Street pickpockets were particularly keen on taking silk handkerchiefs from men's coats because these fetched good prices in the second-hand clothing stalls around Petticoat Lane on the edge of the City of London. The extraction of these was usually the preserve of small boys who were inconspicuous, nimble and dexterous and who were serving an 'apprenticeship' in this trade before perhaps graduating to higher things in the world of robbery.

On the streets of Victorian towns and cities, especially London, begging and thieving were both highly organised operations. Beggars might do a spot of thieving when the opportunity arose, but professional thieves were unlikely to stoop to begging unless with age they had lost their skills and nerve. 'Gegors', professional beggars, showed extraordinary skill and ingenuity in faking the most appalling wounds, sores and suppurating ulcers. Exhibiting these brought them sympathy and, more importantly, money. It was not unknown, for example, for beggars to use vitriol to make sores look more inflamed or to sear the skin and stigmatise themselves with the use of substances like gunpowder. In doing so, they frequently produced real and serious injuries.

False 'blind beggars' had to employ amazing self-control in giving no hint that they were shamming. There is a record of an Irish beggar who worked the country and town fairs and on one occasion latched on to a particularly soft-hearted victim. He poured his heart out to the unsuspecting man, excluding no detail of the ill-treatment he had suffered during his life as a result of his blindness. His new-found friend took all this in and agreed to assist the beggar by taking him to the main highway out of town. Just as they were about to part, the beggar asked the Samaritan if there was anyone else in sight. When he was assured that the road was empty, he suddenly seized his companion, beat him up cruelly, seized all his valuables and made off. He was quickly caught but adamantly stuck to his story that he was blind even when prison staff forcibly tried to prove he was a sham. In court he continued to provide no hint that he was sighted and he was sentenced to be birched. This decision filled him with a thirst for revenge and he was determined to make the magistrate concerned pay for the injustice, and a few weeks later he ambushed him and beat him up with appalling ferocity. Again he was arrested and this time the court was in no doubt that the man had the full use of his eyes.

London has always attracted criminals. Its crowded streets and labyrinthine alleys offered opportunity, anonymity and easy escape. Methods of operation changed but robbers tended to be specialists and frequently developed great skills in the pursuit of their criminal activities. However, the robber on foot in spite of often being daring, ingenious and adroit, never achieved the legendary status that gathered around his mounted counterpart, the highwayman.

FOURTEEN

Jonathan Wild and Jack Sheppard

Jonathan Wild was born in Wolverhampton, Staffordshire, in the early 1680s, the son of a wig-maker according to some accounts, while others say his father was a joiner. He served an apprenticeship as a buckle-maker and married while still a teenager. When aged about twenty-one Wild deserted his wife and child and moved to London. For a while he tried to make an honest albeit unpopular living as a 'bumbailiff' or legal enforcer of writs and summonses. Having already developed a taste for the good things of life, his outgoings exceeded his income and he eventually found himself in the Poultry or Wood Street Compter, where debtors and many other miscreants were housed. He spent four fruitful years in the Compter, meeting a host of influential underworld figures and gaining a thorough and practical knowledge of criminal activity. He carefully stored this information away for future use, becoming convinced that a man who had his wits about him and who knew the right people in London could make himself infinitely richer than if he was to ply an honest trade. In the Compter he became friendly with a prostitute called Mary Millner and, being released at about the same time, he became her pimp. For a time they also engaged in street robbery. Business was brisk and they soon had enough to buy an alehouse at Cripplegate in the City of London where Wild started up additionally as a 'fence' or receiver of stolen goods.

Wild went into partnership with Charles Hitchen, a corrupt City Marshal who doubled as a thief-taker and receiver of stolen goods.

The government of the City of London was corrupt and venal and Hitchen had been able to buy the marshal's job for the then very large sum of £700. This was in the confident expectancy that he would recoup his outlay many times over if he made the maximum use of the opportunities for peculation and graft that the office brought with it. Hitchen was particularly interested in selective street robbery and receiving such items as pocket books and private papers. These had little intrinsic value but may have been particularly treasured by their owners, because they might contain evidence of indiscretions which would therefore make their owners vulnerable to blackmail. The price of such documents was negotiable but when Hitchen had them and those who had been robbed urgently wanted them returned he was definitely well placed. In 1691 and 1706 Parliament had strengthened its powers against receivers who could now be branded, transported or even hanged. As a result, many receivers turned their attentions to other criminal activities. However, street robbery continued unstinted and thieves needed to dispose of the fruits of their labours. Those receivers who had the fortitude to remain in the trade were guaranteed plenty of lucrative business and Hitchen knew this. He was a receiver on a grand scale who controlled gangs totalling 2,000 members. Many of these were teenage boys and he had other interests in them because he was a promiscuous homosexual and regular client at a house of ill-repute known as 'Mother Clap's' in Holborn. Hitchen's business activities and sexual proclivities did not go unnoticed by Wild, who stored the information away for future use. The partnership lasted for nearly two years but Hitchen's indiscretions disconcerted Wild, who was greatly relieved when they quarrelled and went their separate ways.

All thieves faced the problem of how to dispose of their stolen booty. If they took it to a shady pawnbroker they could only expect about a quarter of the value of any stolen item. Receivers were seen as untrustworthy and prepared to save their own skins at any cost. Wild started to exercise his mind on the thorny problem of how to bring about a better working relationship between thieves and receivers. Moll Cutpurse has already been considered (*see* Chapter Five) and just like her, Wild quickly realised that the best way of doing business was to sell stolen goods back to their original owners. Through advertisements and his many contacts Wild soon had people who had been robbed coming into his office, providing a full description of what had been stolen and then willingly paying him to recover their goods for them. He charged a consultation fee of 5s and, in most cases, half his estimate of the market value of the goods, which he was nearly always able to locate very quickly. Street thieves and highwaymen were only too happy to sell him what they had stolen because he always gave them a fair price. Wild was particularly interested in handling personal items such as pocket books, diaries, watches and trinkets because people were often prepared to pay far more than their actual value in order to secure their return.

What made Wild much more successful as a fence than Hitchen, a blustering bully, was that by comparison he exuded sweet reasonableness. He could be very heavy-handed with those who crossed him later on in his career, however. He kept detailed books of his transactions, which included the names of all those he dealt with. He trusted no one and he is supposed to have marked their names with either one or two crosses. One cross denoted that Wild had compiled enough evidence to have the person hanged. A second or double cross was placed against those who he had already or was going to dispose of. Some think that this is the origin of the phrase 'double cross'.

Wild had an uncanny ability to remember faces and names and also the articles that had been negotiated, and he systematically retained this information for possible future use. It was logical to move on to controlling the thieves themselves and their operations. He divided London and its surrounding areas into clearly demarcated districts and assigned individuals or gangs to each. He tolerated no freelance activity by his associates, which is where his

Jack Sheppard's Farewell to Mr Wood.

Blueskin cutting down Jack Sheppard.

The execution of Jack Sheppard, by George Cruikshank. The top section of this illustration shows Sheppard saying farewell to Mr Wood as he arrives at the scaffold at Tyburn. The middle section depicts the cutting down of Sheppard's corpse. The bottom shows the crowd carrying off his body. Sheppard was a good example of a criminal who had won the hearts of Londoners rich and poor, and they turned out en masse to wish him well.

The slippery Jack Sheppard under restraint in Newgate Prison.

The sign at Hopcroft's Holt, Oxfordshire, depicting Claude Duval.

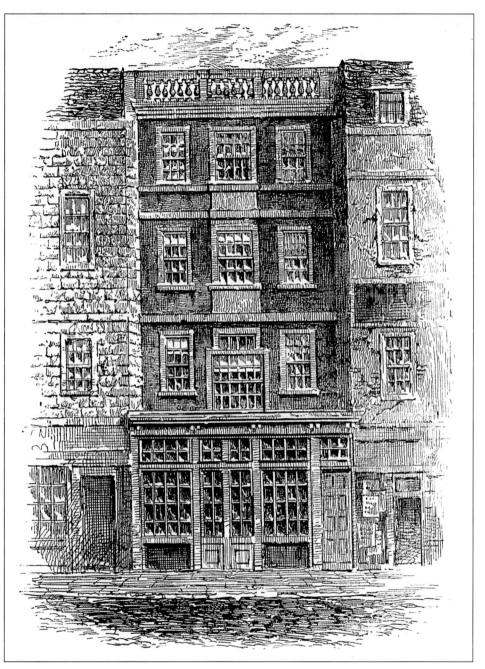

The 'lost property office' operated by Jonathan Wilde, ironically located close to Newgate Prison.

Douglas Fairbanks as Robin Hood in the United Artists film *Robin Hood*, 1922. His swashbuckling portrayal took many liberties with historical facts.

A scene from the Cannon film *The Wicked Lady*, 1983 – the classic evocation of the highwayman, although in this case interest is added by the 'gentler' sex.

prodigious knowledge of their criminal activities as well as their foibles and weaknesses came in extremely useful. Wild was prepared to advance some by encouraging them to specialise in that type of thieving that they did best. Woe betide anyone working for him who became too greedy or the members of rival gangs because Wild was completely ruthless in his dealings with such people. He would go to the authorities and inform them about the criminal activities of those he wanted out of the way, using the information he had painstakingly built up about them. He would agree to act as a prosecution witness and would suborn other witnesses from among his associates whose testimony would see the prisoner at the very least convicted of a felony and therefore unable to testify in court against Wild in the future.

It is obvious that acting in this way, Wild made many enemies and he was assaulted with some frequency. He received two fractured skulls and nearly twenty other wounds. Although small of stature, he was strong and wiry and well able to give good account of himself. Even when temporarily overcome, he would remember his assailant's appearance and character even if the latter were disguised. He would then find some way of settling accounts with him at a later date. He might do this by acting as a thief-taker. This was good business for Wild because he systematically used this to dispose of his enemies, and every time his action secured a conviction he received a reward for doing so. He was an egotistical man and he even went so far as to advertise his services as 'Thief-Catcher General of Great Britain and Ireland'. He also strutted around carrying a baton with a crown on it as a symbol of his office. Wild was becoming exceptionally powerful and dangerous and nobody in London's underworld could afford to offend him. He saw himself going up in the world and therefore parted from Mary and took up with a younger, more attractive woman called Molly and moved to a more prestigious address.

In 1718 Parliament made it a felony to solicit or accept a reward for the return of any stolen property unless information was given as to the identity of the thieves concerned. There is little doubt that this piece of legislation was aimed specifically at Wild and was eloquent testimony to his success as a receiver. His response was to abolish his 5s fee and rename his office 'Enquiry Office for the Recovery of Lost and Stolen Property'. From then on Wild took no money when people came in to describe what they had had stolen. Instead he suggested to them that if they took a specified sum of money to a certain place at a certain time they were likely to find someone there who could restore their property to them. Business boomed. Wild opened branch offices in various parts of London and he even started an export–import business. This involved getting rid of unclaimed goods through Ostend and bringing back smuggled goods, and Wild even bought and fitted out a fine little sloop to assist him in this business. He had several warehouses full of stolen goods that had been plundered by his street robbers and burglars. In these warehouses he employed craftsmen making small alterations to the appearance of watches, jewellery, snuffboxes and other valuables prior to them being sent abroad for sale.

Wild went on to purchase a country seat and to imitate the lifestyle of a landed gentleman, complete with butler, liveried servants and a coach and four. However, such brazen behaviour could not last because Wild had made himself too many enemies both within the legal authorities and among the criminal fraternity. In May 1725, Londoners were shocked but elated to hear that Jonathan Wild had been arrested. He had gone to great lengths to try and render himself legally immune but the authorities had made careful preparations to trap him. He stood trial on two charges. The first was of stealing fifty yards of lace, valued at £40. The second was that he had eventually sold the lace back to its original owner without making any attempt to bring the thief concerned to justice. Clearly this was a test case, and if Wild got away with it he would certainly be completely untouchable in the future. Many other charges against Wild were prepared but not in the event used. He defended himself brilliantly in court and the first charge was dropped. However, he was found guilty of the second charge which infringed the 1718 Act designed with him in mind. He had committed a felony and he was sentenced to death. In vain he displayed the scars from the various injuries he had sustained while engaged in arresting members of the underworld. His plea in mitigation that his activities had led to the prosecution of seventy of London's worst criminals was unsuccessful with judges determined to end his career.

London's population, both the law-abiding and the criminal elements, rejoiced at this unexpected turn of events. At last Wild's reign of terror was over and London prepared to celebrate his procession to Tyburn and his public execution. He nearly cheated the hangman and his hostile audience by taking a large dose of laudanum, but it was insufficient to kill him and so he was forced to run the gauntlet of a vicious torrent of verbal abuse and missiles from a London mob who used the occasion to display their hatred of him. He had no friends that day. A number of accounts of this procession and the actual execution exist but one claims that he at least managed to get something of his own back by picking the pocket of the Ordinary. At this time the Ordinary was a notorious drunkard named the Revd Thomas Purney, and the fact that Wild is supposed to have extracted a corkscrew from his pocket on their journey from Newgate to Tyburn adds authenticity to the story. Wild was buried at St Pancras' Church but was swiftly exhumed because as an executed felon his body had been ordered by a school of anatomy to be used for demonstration purposes. The macabre mystery remains that although a wagon was ordered to take his body away to the school of anatomy, it never got there. The ultimate irony of Wild's life must be that the receiver of this particular piece of stolen goods was never apprehended, nor indeed has the final resting place of his body ever been discovered.

Jonathan Wild was a repulsive character in many ways but for all that he was an intelligent and resourceful gangster, an opportunist who fully exploited the demonstrable weaknesses of the system for maintaining law and order at that time. He became the undisputed leader of London's criminal world and it is possible that, just like the the Kray Brothers, he may actually have made the streets of London safer for ordinary citizens.

Another leading light in the pantheon of London's master-criminals was Jack Sheppard (1702–24) who was prepared to turn his hand to a wide variety of criminal enterprises, including burglary, while specialising as a pickpocket, footpad and highwayman. He owes his fame, however, to his extraordinary skills as an escaplogist from prisons. As with the other criminal characters of this period, it is difficult to disentangle legend from fact. He was a Londoner born in Spitalfields, a vibrant, cosmopolitan, dangerous area on the eastern edge of the City of London. His parents were respectable folk who apprenticed him to a carpenter when he was fifteen. Sheppard could almost be the model for Tom Idle, the 'Idle 'Prentice' in William Hogarth's highly moralistic but popular set of engravings entitled *Industry and Idleness*, published in 1747. Sheppard continued to work in the carpentry trade for four years but then took to carousing with disreputable companions at unsavoury venues such as The Black Lion in Drury Lane. The company to be found there included two questionable women with whom he established an immediate rapport. They were Elizabeth Lyon, also known as 'Edgeworth Bess', and her companion Poll Maggot. They were skilful pickpockets and took Sheppard under their wing, and they found that he quickly became adept at picking the pockets of all sorts of people on the streets of London. However, Sheppard was clearly ambitious because he soon graduated from picking pockets to picking locks, a trade in which the rewards were generally commensurate with the greater skills required.

Eventually Sheppard decided to give up any pretence of pursuing a honest living and he took to the road as a highwayman in the company of the experienced robber Joseph Blake, known as 'Blueskin'. The latter had already carried out a number of commissions for Jonathan Wild and he introduced Sheppard to the master-criminal. It did not take long for Sheppard to establish something of a reputation for himself as a gifted highwayman and he was soon the leader of a gang of villainous ne'er-do-wells that included 'Blueskin' himself. They operated under Wild's overall control, who was impressed by Sheppard because he seems to have given him considerably more latitude than he normally extended to those who worked for him. Gifted highway robber and footpad though he was, Sheppard owes his lasting fame in the annals of criminal history to his remarkable exploits as an escapologist. His first acquaintance with the inside of a prison was when he visited 'Edgeworth Bess' who had been detained while assisting the authorities with their enquiries regarding some missing property. Sheppard resented his ladyfriend's incarceration and knocked out the warder, took his keys and coolly walked out of the building with Bess on his arm. This gained him an instant reputation for devil-may-care audacity and gallantry.

On another occasion Sheppard was strolling through the West End of London with a friend who took a sudden and irresistible liking to the expensive-looking watch sported by a passing gentleman. He tried to snatch the watch but was careless and, realising that he was not going to be able to take it, ran off instantly. Sheppard was surprisingly slow on the uptake and was arrested, for once justifiably protesting his innocence. He was placed in Newgate Prison when who should turn up on his first night but the faithful 'Edgeworth Bess'. The authorities decided that they did not like the look of this demi-rep and so they promptly detained her as a probable accomplice of Sheppard's. This is exactly what the couple wanted because it was assumed that they were man and wife and they were therefore placed in their own cell. This time 'Blueskin' came to their rescue and obtained entry to the gaol as a visitor, managing to pass a file to Sheppard who proved a maestro with this tool. As soon as he deemed it safe, he had his manacles off, followed by his fetters and then two bars were removed from the cell window.

He faced a 30-ft drop into the courtyard below but this was nothing to the intrepid Sheppard. He ripped his blankets and sheets up and knotting them to make a rope, securely attached this to the one window bar still left intact. He descended, followed by Bess stripped to her underwear. Sheppard examined the gaol's outer wall, which was about 22 ft high, but a gate provided convenient footholds and he and Bess duly made their escape.

Perhaps somewhat carried away by this daring escape, Sheppard now made a serious error of judgement. He and 'Blueskin' decided to pursue a little freelance activity and carried out a series of street robberies, passing their booty on to a small-time fence called Field, who offered them far better prices than Wild. The latter soon heard about this and he asked Field to come in and see him. This invitation was not one that could be ignored and Field was persuaded to turn King's evidence, the result of which was that Sheppard and 'Blueskin' were arrested, placed in the dreaded Newgate Prison and soon after put on trial at the Old Bailey. They were found guilty and sentenced to death. Wild decided to visit Newgate to gloat at their downfall, but this nearly proved his undoing. 'Blueskin' approached him, spirited a knife from out of his sleeve and lunged with it at his tormentor's throat, inflicting a very severe wound. For this deed, the date of execution was brought forward. Sheppard meanwhile was making his plans, once again involving the doughty 'Edgeworth Bess' and also Poll Maggot. They were allowed to visit him in gaol but kept apart from him by a hatch through which they could speak but not touch. Bess had secreted a file on her person and deftly manoeuvred it under the hatch with her foot. Poll kept talking to Sheppard while Bess used her wiles to keep the gaolers occupied. Poll and Bess eventually made their way home and Sheppard managed to follow a few days later.

Escapes from Newgate were rare enough to be sensational and his exploits gained Sheppard notoriety in the eyes of the authorities and enormous popularity with the populace at large. He decided to lie low in the countryside for a while but he soon drifted back to his old haunts and habits and was caught equipped for highway robbery on Finchley Common. He was returned to Newgate and this time the authorities, knowing what a slippery character he was, took no chances. They chained him to the floor and refused to allow him any visitors, with or without files. Sheppard was a high-class picklock, however, and he used a crooked nail to open the locks on his chains. He then managed to wriggle out of his handcuffs while still in fetters. He made his way up the only practical exit from the cell which was the chimney. Arriving at the top covered in soot, he climbed out and effected his escape via the roof. His small stature and wiry physique were of enormous help in these escapes. Perhaps continuing success had gone to his head because he decided to celebrate his hard-earned freedom in the company of his faithful friends, Bess and Poll. He dressed in his best finery and brazenly paraded through London in a coach, waving to cheering passers-by before entering an inn to wine and dine. Sheppard had now overreached himself and was quickly arrested, being so drunk as to be totally incapable of resistance.

Back inside Newgate yet again, Sheppard must have rued his vanity but at the same time he was probably flattered because his unusual skills gained official recognition. He was placed in a new set of restraining irons specifically designed for him. This time his luck had run out and Sheppard probably knew it. He continued to be the object of enormous interest and large numbers of visitors, many of them wealthy and female, braved Newgate's noisome stench in order to make his acquaintance as he languished in the condemned cell. However, the warders knew all about his tricks by now and none of these visitors were allowed near him with as much as a toothpick let alone a crooked nail or a file. Such was his celebrity status that artists flocked to paint him, including the Royal Academician Sir James Thornhill. There were even painters who depicted the artists painting Sheppard. Portraits of him in the condemned cell show him to be a delicate, even somewhat effeminate-looking young man of fine features who apparently managed to be unfailingly

181

polite and cheerful through what must have been a very trying time. Skeleton keys and files would really have been more welcome in his situation than all the earnest condolences and commiserations he received. Indeed he is alleged to have said, 'A file is worth all the Bibles in the world.' He was interviewed by Daniel Defoe, who was both a journalist and a Government spy. Defoe produced a somewhat imaginative biography of Sheppard which spawned as many as ten imitations of even more dubious veracity within a year of Sheppard's death.

Somehow or other, the ever resourceful Sheppard managed to acquire a small penknife which he hoped would come in useful as he rode on the cart to Tyburn. If he had tried to escape, it is likely that the crowd would have united to assist him. However, it was not to be because he was frisked by a vigilant gaoler just before he left for his final journey on 16 November 1724. Vast crowds cheered him on his way. He met his death with courage and his remains were buried at St-Martins-in-the-Fields. He was only twenty-two years of age and observers in the crowd were surprised by his look of youthful innocence and vulnerability. In reality there was nothing even slightly upright about Sheppard. Candid accounts from those who knew him but were not selling stories to the press made it clear that he was short-tempered, violent when crossed and that he never displayed any remorse for his crimes. It cannot be denied that he was also intelligent and resourceful and gifted with extraordinary physical and technical skill.

Sheppard as well as being a popular icon was a symbol of the stresses prominent in society during the eighteenth century. He was raised in Spitalfields, perhaps the most intensive centre of industrial activity in Britain at that time, where he would have had first-hand experience of the dynamics and social effects of industrial capitalism in its early stages. He spent time in the workhouse in his childhood. This institution was becoming a major weapon of social control and it institutionalised the degradation and indignity that were heaped on many of the poorest and weakest victims of the economic and social changes taking place during this period. By breaking his indentures, Sheppard became that malevolent and pernicious being, the 'idle apprentice'. 'Idle' meant more than simply lazy, it meant wanton refusal to conform. The establishment of an industrial society in Britain required men, women and children to work in noisy, dangerous factories and to reside in filthy, insanitary slums or austere, inhumane workhouses. Sheppard was idolised because he was not prepared to be treated in this way and because, for a while, he was able to evade or escape from whatever methods the authorities used to try to bring him to heel. The authorities were forced to make an example of Sheppard because he so publicly rejected the attitudes and behaviour required from a compliant working population.

FIFTEEN

Highway Robbers in Literature and Film

In Chapter One the myths and legends surrounding Robin Hood were explored. Probably no other character associated with British folklore has been so celebrated in popular words and song as Robin. The earliest fragments associated with him date back to more than 500 years ago but none of these really obviates the mystery about Robin and his activities. Robin Hood makes an appearance in the narrative poem *Piers Plowman*, written between the 1360s and 1380s, and in several ballads dated from about 1450. He also appears in a variety of fifteenth- and sixteenth-century ritual revels. His green clothing and sylvan associations may have had connections with the 'Green Man' cults and as a fabled outlaw he made an ideal Lord of Misrule. He also received considerable attention from seventeenth- and eighteenth-century antiquaries, such as Joseph Hunter and William Stukeley, and has continued to feature in plays and more recently in films.

In 1908 *Robin Hood and his Merry Men* was released, a British film in which Robin saves a band of his outlaws from the Sheriff of Nottingham's gallows. This was followed in 1912 by *Robin Hood Outlawed*, also a British production. In 1922 the American film *Robin Hood* was issued, which starred Douglas Fairbanks at his buccaneering best, or worst. In 1976 *Robin and Marion* was made, an American film starring Sean Connery, Richard Harris, Audrey Hepburn and Robert Shaw. In it an elderly Robin returns from the crusades to find that his beloved Marion has became an abbess. In

1991 the swashbuckling British film *Robin Hood* was released, starring Patrick Bergin, Uma Thurman, Jurgen Procknow and Edward Fox, while in the same year its American rival *Robin Hood* also came out, featuring Kevin Costner, Morgan Freeman, Sean Connery, Alan Rickman and Elizabeth Mastrantonio. This was not a film for those who preferred their myths to be kept sacrosanct.

One of the earliest films to feature the highwayman theme was *Highwayman Hal*, made in the UK in 1914. This was a comedy starring Harry Buss as Hal Harkaway in which the denouement involves the heroine bringing a pardon from the King at the very last possible moment and thereby saving hero Hal from an ignominious end on the gallows. Other silent films included *A Highwayman's Honour* (1914), *Dick Turpin's Ride to York* with Matheson Lang (1922) and any number of Hollywood versions of Dick Turpin's adventures with such actors as Tom Mix, Victor Mclaglen, Louis Hayward and David Weston in leading roles. Two film adaptations have been made of the story of the highwaywoman Lady Catherine Ferrers, both entitled *The Wicked Lady* and featuring respectively Margaret Lockwood (1945) and Faye Dunaway (1983) in the title role. Laurence Olivier appeared as Macheath in the 1953 film adaptation of *The Beggar's Opera*, while in 1969 Tommy Steele played the lead in *Where's Jack?*, a musical about Jack Sheppard. A British television series in the 1980s featured Richard O'Sullivan as Robin Hood and the theme of highway robbery continues to draw audiences with, for example, Robert Carlyle and Johnny Lee Miller co-starring as *Plunkett and Macleane* (sic), which was screened on network television in April 2000. A film adaptation of Alfred Noyes' poem 'The Highwayman' was filmed in 1951.

Highwaymen have attracted much attention from writers over the centuries. Indeed the writers of fiction have played a major part both in creating and perpetuating the image of romance and gallantry that surrounds the 'Knights of the High Toby'. This literary admiration does not extend to footpads and other forms of criminal life lurking in the streets and highways and the highwayman, therefore, has centre stage even in writing that purports to be factual. A good example of this latter genre is *The History of the Lives of the Most Noted Highwaymen, Footpads, House-breakers, Shop-lifts and Cheats*. This work by Captain Alexander Smith was first published in about 1714 and, in spite of its title, devotes most of its attention to highwaymen. Although it has some factual base, its content is highly impressionistic and subjective. A similar work is Captain Charles Johnson's *General History of the Most Famous Highwaymen*, published in 1734. Other contemporary material can be garnered from such documents as the *Newgate Calendar or Malefactor's Bloody Register*. This was first published in about 1774 and contains anonymous and lurid biographies of the most notorious criminals who spent time confined in Newgate Prison.

Another valuable source is the catchpenny ballads and broadsheets sold, for example, at executions. Although these claim to be factual, much of the material they contain is no more than simple invention and the more lurid and sensational they were the better they sold. A good example of this is *The Life and Death of Gamaliel Ratsey*, published in 1605. This was followed after Ratsey's execution by an even more sensational update, *Ratsey's Ghoste; or, The Second Part of his Madde Pranks and Robberies*. The 'Life and Death' is the earliest recorded biography of a highwayman. Unfortunately, nothing is known of its author or, for that matter, its historical authenticity. A document titled *The Memoirs of Monsieur Du Vall (sic)*, published in 1670, has the subtitle: 'Intended as a severe reflection on the too great fondness of English ladies towards French footmen which at that time of day was a too common complaint'. Although this was once thought to be Duval's autobiography, it was actually written by Dr William Pope. In 1671 Duval's exploits were given fulsome treatment in a panegyric entitled *To the Memory of the Most Renowned Du-Vall* by Samuel Butler (1613–80). The artist William Powell Frith (1819–1909) painted a canvas of the famous tale of Duval dancing with a beautiful and high-born lady before her husband is robbed (*see* Chapter Seven). This well-known work can be viewed in Manchester City Art Gallery.

In 1728 John Gay (1685–1732) produced *The Beggar's Opera*, which was an immediate success, partly because it scandalised polite and puritanical opinion by making heroes of criminals. It features a blackguard by the name of 'Peachum', who is Jonathan Wild under another guise, and the first stage highwayman the gallant 'Captain Macheath', who is in love with Peachum's pretty daughter Polly. Peachum enjoys using the criminals under his control but cares nothing when they have served their purpose and he greedily collects the reward for serving them up to the authorities. The audience enjoys the eventual worsting of the dreadful Peachum and the marriage of Macheath and Polly. Interestingly, Macheath who had been arrested for highway robbery is reprieved, but shows absolutely no remorse for his crimes. These are portrayed as 'social crimes', merely peccadilloes. He can be seen on another level as the popular hero, the maverick who takes up his cudgels for the small people against the all-pervading, all-powerful state that uses tyrants such as Peachum as its agents. Macheath is the prototype of the gallant highwayman-hero and as evidence of nature imitating art, many subsequent highwaymen seem to have thought that they must behave like him. It is highly likely that the part of Macheath was based on James Maclaine.

The authorities deplored the idolisation of a criminal figure and they managed to prevent Gay staging *Polly*, the sequel to *The Beggar's Opera*. They also resented this play because its satirical content unfavourably contrasted the covert corruption and venality of the Government with the open thieving of the highwayman, while also demonstrating that perceptions of wrongdoing are relative. Gay's later operatic drama featuring the life of Jack Sheppard, who was much less successful as a highwayman than as an escapologist from Newgate, was also what we would now consider a box-office success.

Debates have raged for years about the possible corrupting influence on those who watch them of the portrayal of crime and violence on television and in films. It is interesting, therefore, to note that there were two cases of young men from respectable families who claimed to have been so impressed by watching *The Beggar's Opera* that they both resolved to take to lives of crime which, inevitably, ended in the ignominy of a premature death by hanging. But it was not just men who featured in plays about robbery. The female highway robber Ann Meders was immortalised in a seventeenth-century play entitled *The German Princess*, this being her nickname. It was written by John Holden and made something of a sensation in the theatres of London at this time. Samuel Pepys was one celebrity who watched it and it met with his approval.

The glamorised, heroic image of the highwayman was vividly reproduced in Harrison Ainsworth's *Rookwood*. The Dick Turpin that Ainsworth creates here is somewhat eclectic, and the qualities and activities ascribed to Turpin were by no means definitely his own. Ainsworth (1805–82) was a solicitor by profession who found fame and fortune in writing historical novels. These tended to focus on notorious characters from history and included Jack Sheppard and Guy Fawkes. He also produced a fictional work about the seventeenth century goings-on with witchcraft called *The Lancashire Witches*. *Rookwood* appeared in instalments and was enormously successful and was adapted for the theatre and for the circus, as well as being a best-selling novel of the time. As Frank McLynn wittily states about *Rookwood*, '. . . the gallant figure of Dick Turpin is as far removed from the historical personage as an advertising campaign from the tobacco industry is from the truth about lung cancer.'[1]

Ainsworth came under a sustained attack for his novel *Jack Sheppard*, which was published in 1839. This was phenomenally successful, having a major impact not only in its own right but also because of the way in which it generated plagiaristic novels, ballads, plays, periodicals and spurious 'autobiographies' and 'memoirs'. It would be no exaggeration to say that Jack Sheppard, both in an actual historical sense and an imaginative, fictional one, became a cult figure. The novel was reissued in fifteen monthly parts and also many times in complete form. Late in 1839 there were eight plays about him running simultaneously in the theatres of London and untold numbers of loose adaptations of his life being staged in cheap concert rooms attached to drinking places or by street-theatre performers. This runaway success evoked the disapproval of many censorious middle-class Victorians. At this time there was a great belief in the uplifting effects of good books but an even more marked concern about the corrupting effect of 'bad' books on the lower orders, who were thought to be more susceptible to their harmful effects. When Courvoisier, a valet who had brutally murdered his master, admitted in court having read *Jack Sheppard* shortly before he carried out the dastardly deed there was a sustained chorus of 'I told you so'.

Technological advances starting with mechanised paper-making in 1803, the steam press in 1814 and multi-cylinder stereotype printing in 1827 permitted for the first time the cheap and quick dissemination of the printed word. The years between 1830 to 1860 saw a massive rise in the number of journals, magazines and other periodicals of an illustrated and often sensationalised nature and they became an integral part of the evolving popular culture. More ephemeral were the broadsides and chapbooks, many of which were sold by itinerant vendors. A broadside was a single sheet with text and maybe one woodcut illustration which cost a halfpenny or penny at the most. A chapbook was a short, fictional work usually with a soft cover and about a dozen pages, selling for perhaps as much as 3*d*. There was not a great deal of literary merit in these publications but they sometimes sold in surprisingly large numbers, especially if they featured murders and executions. One produced in 1828, giving what was claimed to be the dying speech and confession of the murderer William Corder, sold 1,116,000 copies.

Ballads were an ancient and integral part of popular culture and a valuable method of transmitting ideas from one generation to another. Highwaymen often featured in such material and here are a few excerpts from a piece typical of its genre; the date is unknown:

TURPIN'S VALOUR

On Hounslow Heath, as I rode o'er,
I spied a lawyer riding before;
'Kind sir,' said I, 'are you not afraid,
Of Turpin that mischievous blade?'
O rare Turpin, hero,
O rare Turpin, O.

Says Turpin, 'I have been most acute,
My gold I've hid in the heel of my boot;'
'O,' says the lawyer, 'there's none can find
My gold, for it lies in my cape behind.'
O rare Turpin, hero,
O rare Turpin, O.

As they rode down by the Poulter mill,
Turpin demands him to stand still;
Says he, 'your cape I must cut off,
For my mare she wants a saddle cloth.'
O rare Turpin, hero,
O rare Turpin, O.

For shooting of a dunghill cock,
Poor Turpin he at last was took;
And carried straight into a jail,
Where his misfortune he does bewail.
O poor Turpin hero,
O poor Turpin, O.

> Now Turpin he's condemned to die,
> To hang upon yon gallows high;
> Whose legacy is a strong rope,
> For stealing of a dung-hill cock.
> O poor Turpin hero,
> O poor Turpin, O.

This piece casts Turpin in the usual heroic mode and as a victim of circumstances, although not before he has managed to outwit and rob those usual recipients of popular hatred, lawyers, usurers and excisemen.

Writers of factual rather than fictional material have also had much to say about highwaymen. Thomas de Quincey (1785–1859), best-known for his *Confessions of an Opium Eater*, was not, however, under the influence of drugs when he wrote that highwaymen 'required more accomplishments than either the bar or the pulpit', since they needed to be strong, healthy and agile as well as possessing excellent horsemanship. Writing at about the same time, Thomas Babington Macaulay (1800–59), the noted historian, reiterated the importance of excellent horsemanship skills and remarked that their dashing and romantic activities had great popular appeal.

It is clear from just this sample that the world of the arts in the broadest sense has found a rich seam of inspiration from the activity of highway robbers. The spotlight, however, is firmly on the highwayman and nobody seems to have wanted to celebrate his skulking counterpart, the footpad, in the same way.

SIXTEEN

Some Places Associated with Highwaymen

This list of places in England associated with highwaymen is by no means comprehensive. Tales with or without any basis in fact can be unearthed in every part of the country, and frequently the same story turns up time and time again but in different locations. The common origin may well be an actual event of an especially memorable nature, but the tale has been told and retold, the names of the people and the places involved gradually changed and over a period of many years two or more locations may have claimed to be the place where the famous event took place. What follows is a random sample of the places where these legends are said to have been created.

BEDFORDSHIRE

Aspley Guise

Legend has it that at the old manor Dick Turpin once discovered the corpses of the daughter of the family and her lover, both of which had been shot by the girl's father. He agreed not to inform the authorities in exchange for which he was allowed to use the cellars whenever he needed to take refuge from pursuit. He was also allowed free access to the wine stored there. In Weathercock Lane nearby it is claimed that Turpin's spectre can be seen on an equally ghostly 'Black Bess' riding pell-mell to the manor, but whether intent on hiding or enjoying a few glasses of wine nobody knows.

BUCKINGHAMSHIRE

Beaconsfield

High on the list of tall stories told about highwaymen has to be one about The Crown Inn at Beaconsfield. It is said that Claude Duval was relaxing in the parlour of this establishment when he heard a farmer boasting about all the money he had made at Beaconsfield Fair. He bribed an accomplice, apparently generously, to dress up in cowhide with a pair of horns attached to his head, climb on to the roof and descend the flue into the parlour. This he did, causing a great commotion when he emerged from the fireplace. Many of the already inebriated customers mistook him for the Devil. In the confusion that ensued Duval was able to secure a bag containing £100 from the bragging farmer before slipping away unseen.

Colnbrook

In the middle of the sixteenth century, the ancient pilgrims' inn The Ostrich, was run by John Jarman. He was a highway robber who did not need to go out on the road and thereby run all the risks attached to such activity. In the main guest's room that stood above the brew-house was a bed, the feet of which were nailed to the floor while the mattress was fastened to the bed. This bed stood over a cleverly constructed trap door which could be opened by pulling back the bolts in the brew-house ceiling below. When these bolts were released, the bed tipped up, precipitating its unsuspecting occupant into a large vat of boiling ale directly below. When satisfied that the victim was dead, the landlord and his wife would go through his possessions, removing all the valuables. The genial host then cut the tail and mane of the traveller's horse to change its appearance and sell it to a horse-dealer of flexible morals who never asked embarrassing questions. Back at the inn, enquiries on the whereabouts of the traveller would be answered by saying that he had left in the night without paying his bill, which was not untrue. No useful figure can be given for the number of

Jarman's victims. They range from half a dozen to fifty, a hundred, or more. The body of one victim failed to float away downstream and was identified. Mr and Mrs Jarman had a lot of explaining to do, but nobody was convinced by their story and they were hanged.

CAMBRIDGESHIRE

Near St Neots

At Caxton Gibbet to the east of St Neots among the highway robbers whose mortal remains were set up as an awful testimony to the wages of sin were those of a young man called Gatward. He robbed a postboy journeying from Huntingdon to Royston and he was caught, hanged and gibbeted close to the scene of his crime. There is a story that one night in a storm the gibbet collapsed and a passer-by removed a button from the scarlet coat in which Gatward had been hanged. The button was taken to act as a lucky charm. This is entirely in keeping with the way in which all manner of items associated with hanged felons were considered to be talismans. One landlord of the inn at this site can be justifiably described as a highway robber. He took to thieving from the travellers who stayed there and on one occasion took on three guests all of whom were sleeping in one great bed. He murdered them, tore the rings from their fingers and threw their bodies down a well. There is still a replica gibbet-post nearby and assorted ghosts associated with these dirty deeds are said to appear in the area from time to time.

CHESHIRE

Knutsford

In the centre of the town is the handsome coaching inn, The Royal George. This contains a splendid assembly room as well as bars in which one Henry Higgins used to socialise in his role as a leading light of the town's polite society. However, the debonair and eligible Higgins was not what he appeared to be. When fashionable balls were taking place he often absented himself for a few minutes, entered the ladies' powder room and rifled through the purses, trinkets and other valuables that had been left there. On clear moonlit nights, he would fit woollen socks to his horse's feet to deaden the sound and go off on forays to the neighbouring highways or carry out an occasional burglary. The people of the town were quite amazed when he was identified as a highwayman. He was hanged in November 1767. The attractive house in which Higgins lived still overlooks the Heath, the large expanse of open land adjoining Knutsford's town centre.

DERBYSHIRE

Wardlow Mires

A highwayman called Anthony Lingard was hanged at a nearby crossroads in 1812 for the murder of a widow who was a tollgate-keeper. For this dastardly deed he was gibbeted and his pendent corpse attracted such large crowds of unashamed voyeurs that the local clergyman gave up trying to minister to his flock in the church, cut his losses and took services at the gibbet instead.

DEVON

Near Okehampton

Lewtrenchard Manor in the west of the county is home to the ghost of a highwayman's mother. Captain Edward Gould, nicknamed 'The Scamp', was the young man of the family but was a wastrel, addicted to gambling and in danger of totally frittering away the family fortune, which was substantial. Smarting with humiliation for having incurred especially large losses on one particular occasion, he decided to disguise himself as a highwayman and ambush the man who had won all his money. He waylaid and shot the man, was caught and brought to trial, being defended by an exceptionally able but very expensive barrister by the name of Dunning. The only prosecution witness to the murder claimed that he had recognised Gould by the light of the moon. In response to this, Dunning produced an almanac in court that proved the impossibility of the witness's statement because according to the almanac there was no moon on that night. Gould was discharged. The almanac, however, was a forgery and had been specially drawn up and printed for the trial, although this fact only emerged many years later. The cost of the trial reduced the egregious Gould to poverty in 1777 but his mother used every means possible to ensure that the estate remained in the hands of the family. She was successful, although her hard work was at the cost of her own life. She loved Lewtrenchard Manor and her presence in the form of a benevolent ghost remains there to this day.

ESSEX

Epping Forest

This area practically groans under the weight of the Turpin legends. However, Turpin and his associate Tom King were not the only robbers who used the forest as a base. In 1698 a dangerous gang of ex-soldiers robbed, assaulted and murdered travellers on the Cambridge and Newmarket roads. Unsuccessful attempts were made to suppress this gang, which mocked these efforts to the extent of sending a letter of defiance to the Government. Eventually, a powerful detachment of dragoons was despatched to Epping Forest and they successfully rooted them out and destroyed them. Close to Theydon Bois on the edge of the Forest is a pub called Sixteen-String Jack, so named in memory of Jack Rann, the dandy of all highwaymen.

Hempstead

In The Rose and Crown, Dick Turpin's birthplace, a copy of his birth certificate can be seen. Opposite the pub is a group of great oak trees known as 'Turpin's Ring'.

HAMPSHIRE

Crondall near Farnham

In Alma Lane the sound of someone running in heavy boots can be heard. This is reputed to be the ghost of a messenger who was bringing news of the wonderful victory at Waterloo in 1815 but was then rather ungraciously stopped, robbed and murdered by a gang of footpads.

Liphook

The Royal Anchor Hotel was used as a base for the depredations of highwayman 'Captain Jacques', who operated along the Portsmouth Road. This hotel had a maze of secret rooms and Jacques came to a bloody end while desperately trying to open a hidden door in a fireplace. Had he been successful, he would have gone down a secret staircase to the cellar, under the main square of the town and up into the bar of another of the town's inns. It would only have been a matter of waiting until the bar was quiet and then emerging, getting out of the building and away. On this occasion, his intentions were fatally thwarted.

HERTFORDSHIRE

Boxmoor Common

Close to the road from Berkhamsted to London stands a stone that marks the burial place of Robert Snooks, said to be the last highwayman to be hanged in England, on 11 March 1802.

Hitchin

In 1772 two robbers, described as highwaymen broke into The Sun Inn and robbed the patrons and the landlord at gunpoint. On their way out they scratched their initials in brickwork by the main door and these initials can still be seen today.

Markyate Cell

This was the base from which the infamous Lady Ferrers used to emerge at night to rob travellers on the local roads. It is said that she sometimes tethered her horse, climbed up into a tree with branches that overhung the highway and dropped on to her victims. This method of attack alone puts her in a class of her own. One night she was shot and mortally wounded by one of her intended victims and she got home only to collapse and die as she reached the door. Her ghost is said to haunt the area around Markyate Cell. Her figure is seen riding hell-for-leather across the countryside, jumping fences, lurking in a number of suitable trees and also passing through the garden of Markyate Cell itself. Lady Ferrers is reputed to have amassed a fortune and local legend has it that this little rhyme gives a clue to where it is to be found:

> Near the Cell, there is a well,
> Near the well, there is a tree,
> And 'neath the tree, the treasure be.

No one has yet found the treasure.

KENT

Fright Corner, Dering Wood near Pluckley

The sinister ghost of a highwayman is seen here, reputedly run through with a sword by his intended victim and impaled to a tree.

In this case the ghost seems to have managed to detach himself from both tree and sword because the galloping hoofs of his horse are heard and he is glimpsed riding at full tilt as if his very life depends on it.

LANCASHIRE

Hurst Green

Hurst Green is a small settlement in the lovely Ribble Valley not far from Whalley and in about 1800 a highwayman lived there. He used a spyhole in a barn overlooking the yard of The Punchbowl Inn to estimate the wealth of the travellers who stopped there for hospitality. Satisfied that he had a rich one within his sights, he would then ride off and ambush him at a suitably lonely spot not too far away. Unluckily for him, in recognition of his success, the authorities put a price on his head and an informer revealed where he could be found. He was trapped in the barn, seized, carried away in irons and subsequently hanged.

LEICESTERSHIRE

Wigston

George Davenport was a popular man in this small town south of Leicester and when he turned highwayman, making no secret of the fact, local people regarded his activities as peccadillos rather than the crimes they actually were. The locals particularly admired his trick of making friends with recruiting sergeants, getting them drunk and then stealing their horses. One day, however, he was out on the road and he called on a butcher to stop and render. This man was so incensed by this impudent request that he clubbed Davenport over the head, knocked him out and personally dragged him in front of the magistrate. Davenport was sentenced to death but he went out in style. To applause and huzzas from an appreciative crowd, he borrowed a chaise and pair and insisted on driving himself to the gallows just outside Leicester.

LONDON

Hampstead Heath

The Spaniards Inn is haunted by the ghost of Dick Turpin and the hoofbeats of 'Black Bess' can be heard. The pub contains Turpin memorabilia including the leg-irons in which he was reputedly shackled while awaiting execution. There is a small and apparently unnecessary tiny window on a staircase through which it is said that food was passed to Turpin when he was lying low at the inn. So many pubs claim associations with Turpin that it would appear that most of his life was spent carousing in convivial inns. On hearing the hue-and-cry, he would leap out of an upstairs window to land with consummate skill in the saddle of the faithful ever-patient and fleet-of-foot 'Black Bess'. As she carried him off into the great blue yonder those who knew Turpin must have wondered how he ever found the time for highway robbery.

Knightsbridge

Here the road westwards out of London forded the Westbourne stream and travellers had to slow down and indeed often got stuck in the mud churned up at this busy point, which remained largely rural as late as the early nineteenth century. The location attracted highwaymen and it was particularly mortifying for travellers into London if they had crossed Hounslow Heath unscathed only to be robbed so close to the city. Sometimes highwaymen were gibbeted at this point and among those whose gory remains once looked down on travellers was William Hawkes, 'The Flying Highwayman'.

Tyburn

The actual site of the gallows at Tyburn is now marked with a circular plaque set into the traffic island at the bottom of the Edgware Road, close to Marble Arch. The old 'Triple Tree' on which so many highwaymen and other highway robbers came to a wretched end had one leg in each of three adjoining parishes, these being St Georges's in Hanover Square, St Marylebone and Paddington.

MIDDLESEX

Hounslow .

The Bath and Exeter Roads and the way to Windsor, where the King frequently held court, made their way across Hounslow Heath. It was one of the busiest places on Britain's roads and it attracted large numbers of highway robbers. A line of gibbets was erected on the Heath to act as deterrents to robbers but there is little evidence that such gory sights had the effect for which they were intended. In 1899 when an electric tramway was being built, the stumps of these gibbet posts were unearthed. Close to Hounslow Heath an Irish bishop by the name of Twysden died from gunshot wounds strongly suggesting that he had been acting as a highwayman. However, to smooth possible ruffled feathers, it was said that he had died of an 'inflammation'.

OXFORDSHIRE

Hopcroft's Holt

The pub in this village claims to have been used by Claude Duval. The sign depicts Duval himself along with a gibbet and a noose, while his ghost is said to wander about the place from time to time.

Shipton-under-Wychwood

An old oak tree stands near the former inn known as Capp's Lodge. Just visible on this tree are the carved initials 'H.D.' and 'T.D.' with the date '1784'. These refer to Harry and Tom Dunsdon who were highwaymen. A third brother, Dick, is said to have bled to death when Tom and Harry hacked off one of his arms to free him. It had been grasped by waiting constables when he had reached through a door shutter to slide back the bolt. They were both hanged at Gloucester in 1784.

SOMERSET

Cannard's Grave Inn, near Shepton Mallet

This inn stands at the intersection of five roads and at one time had a landlord called Cannard. He was not content with the income he received as a publican and enriched himself by organising gangs of highway robbers and also by acting as a receiver. He became too ambitious and started dabbling in forgery and then realised that the authorities were on to him for crimes that carried the death penalty. He was unwilling to give himself up and so he hanged himself and was buried at the crossroads close to where he and his robbers had operated. His grisly death is commemorated in the signboard for the pub and a spectral Cannard has frequently been seen in the area.

Winsford

The Royal Oak at Winsford has associations with Tom Faggus, a notorious highwayman who was probably a dispossessed Royalist and ex-soldier. His fame was such that the novelist R.D. Blackmore saw fit to make him a character in the most famous of his novels, *Lorna Doone*, which was published in 1869.

SUFFOLK

Nayland

Monuments to highwaymen in burial grounds are few and far between. However, there is one in the churchyard at Nayland, in medieval times a wool town but now scarcely more than a village. The highwayman was called Edward Alston, who actually carried out most of his robberies outside Suffolk. The memorial is a punning one:

> My friend, here I am – Death has at last prevailed,
> And for once all my projects are baffled.
> 'Tis a blessing in disguise to know,
>   though, when once a man's nailed,
> He no longer has fear of the scaffold.
> My life was cut short by a shot through the head
> On His Majesty's highway at Dalston;
> So now 'Number One's' numbered one of the dead
> All's one if he's Alston or all-stone.

SURREY

Bagshot Heath

William Davis, also known as the 'Golden Farmer', was particularly associated with Bagshot Heath, which in the days of the highwaymen was a particularly lonely and inhospitable spot. A local pub was called The Golden Farmer but someone with little sense of history changed its name to the more prosaic, even banal, Jolly Farmer. Davis, incidentally, was commemorated in a contemporary ballad called 'The Golden Farmer's Last Farewell' which was adapted as a play and staged as late as 1832.

Ripley

Claude Duval was a frequent visitor at The Talbot Inn at Ripley. He used to stay overnight and he always booked into the same room from which he could make a quick escape if necessary via a chimney and the back door.

WARWICKSHIRE

Gaydon

The Gaydon Inn was used by stagecoaches and other travellers in the eighteenth century. It was also the headquarters of the notorious and brutal Culworth Gang who came from the village of Culworth just over the border in Northamptonshire. Among their victims were farming folk, often people they knew personally, returning from market having had a lucrative day. On one occasion they took £450 from just three farmers. They used the inn for planning their robberies and dividing the spoils but were eventually brought to justice in 1787 because the drunken indiscretions of one of the gang were overheard by a public-spirited citizen.

WILTSHIRE

Chippenham

Near this Wiltshire town on the Bath Road a naked footpad was known to operate.

YORKSHIRE

Giggleswick

Law enforcers were apparently closing in on 'Swift Nicks' Nevison who local legend says evaded capture by letting his horse drink at the nearby 'Ebbing and Flowing Well'. His horse was so invigorated by the waters that it spirited Nevison away and out of the reach of his pursuers by dramatically leaping over the cliff still known as 'Nevison's Leap'.

SEVENTEEN

Conclusion

John Locke (1632–1704) in writings such as *An Essay Concerning Human Understanding* and *Two Treatises of Government* acts as the ideological and intellectual mouthpiece of the emerging industrial and mercantile classes for whom the acquisition, possession and protection of property was sacrosanct. He equated the preservation of property with the common good and argued, with disarming frankness, that the purpose of political power was to make laws and create a system of legal penalties up to and including death in order to regulate and protect private property. Highway robbers were equally dedicated to the idea of private property but from a very different standpoint.

The golden era of the highwayman coincided with crucial stages in the process that transformed Britain from a pre-industrial, largely rural and agricultural economy into an urban, manufacturing, commercial and trading nation. In this process, known as the Industrial Revolution, there were far-reaching changes in land use and agriculture, the nature and development of industry, the employment, living and cultural patterns of the ordinary people and the political and legal framework in which property and social relations were embedded. It saw the completion of the process whereby capitalist methods came to dominate economic activity in Britain. The triumph of capitalism unleashed processes that created untold wealth but for which a high price had to be paid. The creation of this new society was carried through without the active consent of the bulk of the population and the period 1700 to 1850 is punctuated with examples of individual and collective protest as ordinary people demonstrated their hostility to the changes that were being made to so much of what they were familiar with.

The concept of the modern State evolved, an impartial arbiter between the interests of the various classes in society. To the State was arrogated the monopoly of legitimate internal violence. It was argued that this was available for use against those malevolent elements who sought to undermine the stability and welfare of society but this can be read to mean the rights of property and profits. The 'Rule of Law' therefore was used to legitimate established property relations and was portrayed as an impartial agency available to each and every citizen equally. In practice it was concerned first and foremost with the protection of property. Most people had none.

In the course of the Industrial Revolution the poor had their means of production appropriated as they mainly became landless labourers or industrial workers, a wage-earning proletariat. The fact that they resented this process is evident from the songs and ballads prevalent during the early nineteenth century and from the vast amounts of protest activity that took place. A clear articulation of the stresses created by these processes was confined largely to the more literate members of the working classes and some middle-class sympathisers. However, it is not surprising that people who saw their way of life coming under relentless attack made heroes of those who appropriated the property of the rich and did so with the panache so often ascribed to highwayman.

A surprising number of butchers seem to have become highwaymen and this may be explained by the fact that capitalist forms of organisation were brought into the meat industry comparatively early. Butchers found themselves reduced to the status of mere shopkeepers in a trade where supply, distribution and retailing were increasingly in the hands of large national concerns who dominated the industry and were able to dictate the terms under which butchers operated. Butchers can be seen as a microcosm of the kind of changes taking place in the eighteenth and nineteenth centuries. These rained down on ordinary people, on the way they made their living and every other aspect of their lives. Many felt powerless and some, including butchers, cast round for an alternative. In a largely unconscious defiance of the rich and powerful and their market forces and laws, some of them turned to highway robbery. Even among those that did not express the resentment they felt in this way, there was widespread admiration for highwaymen.

To become a highwayman was to make a personal statement about wanting to be a somebody, a freebooter, a person prepared to take control of his life and to use the power that went with a pair of pistols. It was also to defy the law to do its worst. The ballads and broadsides of the period give an insight into what ordinary folk thought about the events happening. It is probably no coincidence that the popularity of ballads about Robin Hood and the various eulogistic portrayals of highwaymen seem to have reached a height at the time when the impact of the Industrial Revolution was being felt with its full force. The carefree lives apparently led by the Robin Hoods and Dick Turpins of the world must have been contrasted with the drab, oppressive existence of the rural and urban labourers and their families. These people would have warmed, for example, to the actions of the Wiltshire highwayman Benjamin Child. In the early 1720s he carried out a series of audacious and profitable robberies and then used the proceeds to buy a number of debtors out of Salisbury Gaol. A few years earlier the self-styled 'Captain' Evan Evans and an accomplice were lying in wait for travellers on the Portsmouth Road. Along came a party of woebegone wretches swept up by the hated press-gang. Evans and his partner attacked the escort, tied them to a tree and released all their prisoners. As the liberated men disappeared swiftly and gratefully to all points of the compass, another page was written in the popular annals of the highwaymen heroes.

Conclusion

Social bandits who enjoy widespread support among the populace are products of periods when the equilibrium of society is upset and long-established and reassuring practices and customs are destroyed. The society of the eighteenth century was violent, corrupt and greedy and these traits were personified by the highwayman. He was at least open about it, but by contrast thousands of politicians and placemen used their positions to line their pockets and did so behind a veneer of authority and respectability. Highwaymen and other highway robbers went to their deaths for stealing what were frequently paltry sums while a politician like Sir Robert Walpole peculated to the tune of hundreds of thousands of pounds during his career. Soon after Jack Sheppard was hanged for his crimes against society, the Earl of Macclesfield, who had been Chancellor at the time, was impeached and subsequently dismissed from office for bribery and embezzlement to the tune of £100,000. He never stood trial for theft. Was there any significant qualitative difference between the violent expropriation of a rich man's property by a robber on a horse and the legally sanctioned and forcible seizure of commons and wasteland by enclosure that deprived so many people of their living on the land? While the answer to this question may be no, the mystery, glamour and fascination accorded to highwaymen gives them a remarkable place in history.

Notes

Chapter One

1. M. Murray, *The God of the Witches*, London, 1933.
2. C. Hole, *English Folk Heroes*, London, Batsford, 1948.
3. E.J. Hobsbawm, *Bandits*, 2nd edn, London, Penguin, 1985.

Chapter Two

1. Quoted in J.J. Jusserand, *English Wayfaring Life in the Middle Ages*, London, University Paperbacks Edition, Methuen, 1961, p. 77.

Chapter Eleven

1. J. Pearson, quoted in D. Rumbelow, *I Spy Blue*, London, Macmillan, 1971, pp. 57–8.
2. L. Radzinowicz, *A History of English Criminal Law and its Administration*, 5 vols, London, Stevens, 1948–86, p. 327.

Chapter Twelve

1. Quoted in D. Rumbelow, *The Triple Tree. Newgate, Tyburn and Old Bailey*, London, Harrap, 1982, p. 170.
2. Quoted in V.A.C. Gattrell, *The Hanging Tree. Execution and the English People, 1770–1868*, New York, Oxford University Press, 1994, p. 60.
3. Quoted in Rumbelow, *The Triple Tree*, p. 194.
4. Quoted in D. Cooper, *The Lesson of the Scaffold. The Public Execution Controversy in Victorian England*, London, Allen Lane, 1974, pp. 20–1.

Chapter Fifteen

1. F. McLynn, *Crime and Punishment in Eighteenth-Century England*, Oxford, Oxford University Press, 1991, p. 57.

Bibliography

Anderson, P. *The Printed Image and the Transformation of Popular Culture, 1790–1860*, Oxford, Oxford University Press, 1991

Anderson, R.C. and Anderson, J.M. *Quicksilver. A Hundred Years of Coaching. 1750–1850*, Newton Abbot, David & Charles, 1973

Anglo, M. *Man Eats Man. The Story of Cannibalism*, London, Jupiter, 1979

Ash, R. *Discovering Highwaymen*, 2nd edn, Princes Risborough, Shire Publications, 1994

Ayedelotte, F. *Elizabethan Rogues and Vagabonds*, Oxford, Clarendon Press, 1913

Babington, A. *A House on Bow Street. Crime and the Magistracy, 1740–1881*, London, Macdonald, 1969

Bagwell, P.S. *The Transport Revolution*, London, Batsford, 1974

Barrows, J. *Knights of the High Toby. The Story of the Highwaymen*, London, Peter Davies, 1962

Billett, M. *Highwaymen and Outlaws*, London, Cassell, 1997

Briggs, J., Harrison, C., McInnes, A. and Vincent, D. *Crime and Punishment in England*, London, UCL Press, 1996

Burford, E.J. *London The Synfulle Citie*, London, Robert Hale, 1990

Burke, T. *Travel in England*, London, Batsford, 1942

Chesney, K. *The Victorian Underworld*, London, Pelican, 1972

Cooper, D.D. *The Lesson of the Scaffold. The Public Execution Controversy in Victorian England*, London, Allen Lane, 1974

Davey, B.J. *Rural Crime in the Eighteenth Century*, Hull, Hull University Press, 1994

Dyos, H.J. and Aldcoft, D.H. *British Transport*, Leicester, Leicester University Press, 1971

Emsley, C. *Crime and Society in England, 1750–1900*, 2nd edn, London, Longman, 1996

——. *The English Police. A Political and Social History*, 2nd edn, London, Longman, 1996

Bibliography

Evans, H. and M. *Hero on a Stolen Horse*, London, Frederick Muller, 1977

Gattrell, V.A.C. *The Hanging Tree. Execution and the English People, 1770–1868*, New York, Oxford University Press, 1994

George, M.D. *London Life in the Eighteenth Century*, Peregrine edn, London, Pelican Books, 1966

Haining, P. *The English Highwayman. A Legend Unmasked*, London, Robert Hale, 1991

Hanson, H. *The Coaching Life*, Manchester, Manchester University Press, 1983

Hay, D., Linebaugh, P., Rule, J.G., Winslow, C. and Thompson, E.P. *Albion's Fatal Tree. Crime and Society in Eighteenth Century England*, London, Penguin, 1977

Hibbert, C. *Highwaymen*, London, Weidenfeld & Nicolson, 1967

——. *The Road to Tyburn. The Story of Jack Sheppard and the Eighteenth Century Underworld*, London, Longmans, 1977

Hobsbawm, E.J. *Bandits*, 2nd edn, London, Penguin, 1985

——. *Primitive Rebels*, 3rd edn, Manchester, Manchester University Press, 1971

Holt, J.C. *Robin Hood*, 2nd edn, London, Thames and Hudson, 1989

Howson, G. *It Takes a Thief. The Life and Times of Jonathan Wild*, London, Cresset, 1987

Hughes, R. *The Fatal Shore*, London, Pan Books, 1988

Hutton, R.A. *The Rise and Fall of Merry England*, Oxford, Oxford University Press, 1996

Linebaugh, P. *The London Hanged. Crime and Civil Society in the Eighteenth Century*, London, Penguin, 1991

Low, D.A. *Thieves' Kitchen. The Regency Underworld*, London, J.M. Dent & Sons, 1982

Lyons, F.J. *Jonathan Wild. Prince of Robbers*, London, Michael Joseph, 1936

McCall, A. *The Medieval Underworld*, London, Hamish Hamilton, 1979

McLynn, F. *Crime and Punishment in Eighteenth-Century England*, Oxford, Oxford University Press, 1991

Moore, L. *The Thieves' Opera. The Remarkable Lives and Deaths of Jonathan Wild, Thief Taker, and Jack Sheppard . . .*, London, Viking, 1997

Morris, N. and Rothman, D.J. (eds). *The Oxford History of the Prison. The Practice of Punishment In Western Society*, New York, Oxford University Press, 1995

Newark, P. *The Crimson Book of Highwaymen*, London, Jupiter, 1979

Palmer, R. *The Sound of History. Songs and Social Comment*, Oxford, Oxford University Press, 1988

Paulson, R. *The Art of Hogarth*, London, Phaidon, 1975

Pearson. G. *Hooligan. A History of Respectable Fears*, London, Macmillan, 1983

Philips, D. 'Crime, Law and Punishment' in *The Industrial Revolution and British Society*, eds P.K. O'Brien and R. Quinault, Cambridge, Cambridge University Press, 1993

Pringle, P. *Stand and Deliver. The Story of the Highwaymen*, London, Museum Press, 1951

——. *Hue and Cry. The Birth of the British Police*, London, Museum Press, 1955

——. *The Thief Takers*, London, Museum Press, 1958

Rule, J. *Albion's People. English Society, 1714–1815*, London, Longman, 1992

Rumbelow, D. *I Spy Blue. The Police and Crime in the City of London from Elizabeth I to Victoria*, London, Macmillan, 1971

——. *The Triple Tree. Newgate, Tyburn and Old Bailey*, London, Harrap, 1982

Salgado, G. *The Elizabethan Underworld*, London, J.M. Dent & Sons, 1977

Sharpe, J.A. *Crime in Early Modern England, 1550–1750*, London, Longman, 1984

Sparkes, I. *Stagecoach and Carriages. An Illustrated History of Coaches and Coaching*, Bourne End, Spurbooks, 1975

Tannahill, R. *Flesh and Blood. A History of the Cannibal Complex*, London, Hamish Hamilton, 1975

Thomas, D. *The Victorian Underworld*, London, John Murray, 1998

Thompson, E.P. *The Making of the English Working Class*, London, Penguin, 1968

——. *Whigs and Hunters. The Origins of the Black Act*, London, Peregrine, 1977

Tobias, J.J. *Crime and Industrial Society in the Nineteenth Century*, London, Pelican, 1967

Walvin, J. *English Urban Life, 1776–1851*, London, Hutchinson, 1984

Index

Index